Murunna Point Revisited

Ian McFarlane is an award-winning author, essayist and critic He lives near Bermagui on the far south coast of NSW with his wife, Mary.

Also by Ian McFarlane

The Jerusalem Conspiracy

The Siberian Sparrows

Shadows

Of Cheese and Chutney

The Shapes of Light

Aspects of Empathy (Pocket Poets)

The Final Straw (Pocket Poets)

A Bold Concept (Pocket Polemics)

Of Bluebells and Barbed Wire (Pocket Places)

Ian McFarlane

Murunna Point Revisited

Murunna Point Revisited
ISBN 978 1 76041 292 0

Cover photo: Gulaga from Murunna Point, Ian McFarlane

First published 2017 by
GINNINDERRA PRESS
PO Box 3461 Port Adelaide 2617
www.ginninderrapress.com.au

Contents

The Black Dog of clinical depression was once called the sin of accidie, and known to 'attack the monk at the fourth hour'. Whatever the name, it occupies a world of such chilling isolation that its reality rests far beyond the imagination of anyone who doesn't know the landscape. I do, having lived there for so long it seems like home.

To those few friends who have, over the years, bothered to visit without worrying about the stony path and heavy gate, these essays, stories and poems are gratefully dedicated.

These wines can so deceive us
They lift us as we cling
How far it is to happiness
Beyond remembering.

– John Shaw Neilson

Introduction

Life is a work in progress, usually assumed to be in final draft, but constantly revised by the vagaries of circumstance. When *Evening at Murunna Point* was first published in 2001, the world was on the dreadful cusp of a human error, involving age-old conflicts sufficiently unhinged to allow the absurdity of declaring war on an abstract noun. The risibly named War on Terror was conjured from a criminally reckless invasion of Iraq in 2003, which in turn was motivated by revenge, sanctioned by lies and perpetuated by arrogance. The ongoing cost of this stupendous folly – in human as well as monetary terms – continues to accrue, like aggressively applied compound interest, with increasingly tragic side effects, including the self-fulfilling prophecies of security paranoia, and the monstrous injustice of treating refugee families as if they were common felons, rather than innocent victims trying to flee a nightmare that we helped to create.

Iraq, Syria and Afghanistan are now ruined states, as the chaotic legacy of religious, ethnic and cultural hatreds come home to roost. As I write these words, global politics, poisoned by Islamic minority extremism and right-wing Christian arrogance, is a watch-this-space daily proposition, while a shallow and disingenuous Australian government, effectively paralysed by ideological bickering and a hostile Senate, stumbles backwards mouthing tedious slogans about moving forward. In essence, humanity today occupies a possibly final battle ground between fear and hope, and since fear is the more powerfully contagious emotion, our tired old world teeters towards catastrophe; which, apart from anything else, is achingly sad, because – with genuine good will and honestly collective application – it could all be so very different.

As a shy and sceptical child, growing up in England in the shadow of World War II, I was already inclined towards sadness; too easily spooked into anxiety by injustice, and apt to seek refuge in solitude. As a jittery young adult in Canberra, the bush capital of Australia, seeking a moral foothold in the chaos of helping to raise a young family while studying to repair an interrupted education, I guess it was hardly surprising to stumble upon the waking nightmare of what is still carelessly dismissed as nervous breakdown.

In fact, it was merely the foothills; a terrifyingly inexplicable panic attack, involving the utter conviction that I was being suffocated by a brutal but invisible force. I knew nothing back then about hyperventilation triggered by accumulated stress, and my doctor, a busy suburban GP, was unable – or disinclined – to enlighten me as he scribbled a script for tranquillisers, and muttered a few side of the mouth words about wasting his time. He should have known – as I do now – that where you have unresolved anxiety, there, sooner or later, you will have clinical depression. And so it came to pass, eventually creating the catastrophe of a fully-fledged breakdown that robbed me of a Foreign Service administrative career to which I was well-suited, and at which I was occasionally rather good.

Evening at Murunna Point was launched with the customary empathy of Ginninderra Press publisher Stephen Matthews in 2001, and well received. Four years later, a metal plaque containing the final stanza of its title poem was fitted to a seat on the headland overlooking Murunna Point, at the entrance to Wallaga Lake. Approved by local authorities, as well as the Yuin people, Indigenous Australians for whom Murunna Point has special cultural significance, the occasion was marked by a ceremonial welcome dance, performed by Aboriginal children, and watched by a few of my friends, including a couple of fellow poets. As I read a poem under a blue sky canvas haunted by hastily daubed clouds, and thanked everyone for taking part in finding a home for a stanza of verse acknowledging the ancient beauty of a sacred site, I remember hoping that our little cross-cultural ceremony might have touched, if only for a brief few moments, a distant corner stone of reconciliation.

I've always believed in the socially relevant healing properties of books and writing, and through my long and lonely personal struggle with a mostly invisible illness, I have gathered evidence in support of this belief. Clinical depression is a malignant mystery, and although public perception has improved since my distant ambush by hyperventilation, there is still far to go.

In bringing *Evening at Murunna Point* into the digital age, I have taken the opportunity to replace some of the early edition material with several new stories, essays and poems, in the hope of helping to find some compass points. For example, I still cling to my belief that poetry holds a useful key to social and cultural cohesion, despite a lingering inner circle presumption that accessibility rests with the person approaching the poem rather than the person offering it. While this may be the case in some specialised areas, a wider notion is mostly arrogant nonsense. Released from the precious exclusions of a few gatekeepers, creative imagination generally – and poetry specifically – can provide a universally humanising art. And while I certainly wouldn't make that claim on behalf of my own work, now is the time, if ever there was one, to reach for a more inclusive creative community.

Ian McFarlane

Wallaga Lake, NSW, 2017

Preface

> A man who is unable to despair
> has no need to be alive.
>
> – Goethe

Near the entrance to Wallaga Lake, a few kilometres north of Bermagui on the far south coast of NSW, there's a path that winds through a grove of crowded melaleucas and twisted eucalypts stunted by the wind before opening onto a small, cave-like clearing, with dramatic cliff-top glimpses of the sea. At dusk the place has the eerie resonance of half-remembered bedtime stories, and a scary kind of pagan spirituality. Alone on the path in fading light – as is my wont – I sometimes glance over my shoulder, half expecting to see goblins, or a vaguely human shape clutching a pan-flute disappear into the tangled trees. Murunna Point is a song of enchantment in a disenchanted world. As far removed from cyberspace as poetry is from economic rationalism. It's a dreamtime place.

As a book reviewer, I know the dangers of diminishing a text by defining it, which is why I'm prepared to accept that places like Murunna Point are important to our sense of humanity without banging around looking for too many reasons. Technology has sent us on a quest for the Holy Grail of mathematical, economic and sociological explanations, but as the American mystic poet, Emily Dickinson, said, 'Life is a spell so exquisite that everything conspires to break it.'

Language is a powerful magic, but sadly it's been corrupted and trivialised by the awesome age of digital social media. I'm no Luddite; I don't want to smash every computer and beat back cyberspace, but the digital age has disenchanted us, and the human psyche needs enchantment as the body needs water. The Latin root of the word 'author' is argument, and that's what writers do: argue a case. Let me argue mine by quoting the German poet, Friedrich Holderlin, who would have had no trouble recognising the enchantment of Murunna

Point: 'I was raised by the song of the murmuring grove, and loving I learned among flowers.'

Winston Churchill, echoing Sam Johnson and others even earlier, referred to his depression as the black dog. It's a beast that can savage anyone, although evidence suggests that writers and artists are at greater risk, perhaps because they're inclined to look at reality closer than most other people. When Vincent van Gogh carved off his ear, and Virginia Woolf, Sylvia Plath and Ernest Hemingway snuffed out their lives, they did so because existence had become unbearable. Reality had shrivelled to a one-dimensional, unbalanced focus, trapped behind invisible walls. They were depressed. Not all such people achieve self-annihilation by mutilating or killing themselves. Many do so in curiously remote and non-violent ways, as medievalist poet, John Donne, suggests with the chilling line 'But I do nothing upon myself, and yet am mine own executioner.'

A very depressing thing about depression is the routine way it's so easily misunderstood; of course, there are levels of sadness and sorrow that fluctuate throughout all our lives, but the desolation of clinical depression is horrifyingly unique; as far removed from sadness, feeling low, or having a bad day, as cancer is from a chest cold. At its darkest core, there's a sense of loneliness which is virtually indefinable, but something akin to being sent into exile without leaving home. Unless you've experienced it first hand, you can have no inkling of the black dog's ferocity, but multiplying your worst nightmare by a factor of ten might get you close. Depression is metaphysical pain that can cripple its victim as effectively as physical injury. But remains invisible to everyone other than the afflicted.

I do what I do – write book reviews, fiction, essays, and poetry – only by dint of enormous and utterly exhausting effort. Depression is writers' block with a tonne of lead ballast. Interaction with other people – even friends and family – becomes difficult. I have to work very hard to do the routine, everyday things most people take for granted; like helping with the groceries, meeting up with friends, or even playing a much-loved game of tennis. Depression is a thief; it robs you of the things you most enjoy. At school, and as a young man, I was a promising chess player, but playing chess now is how I'd imagine a sprinter would feel trying to run with a fractured ankle. I must carry the pain of the depression experience itself, as well as the additional burden of knowing that even the people closest to me will never fully understand the degree of its handicap.

The black dog has loped along behind me, snapping at my heels, for most of my life. Occasionally he falls back but never lets me forget that he is there. If I turn and stare him straight in the eye, he hesitates and seems to lose his way, but never disappears. For as long as I can remember, the panic-fear likely to accompany depression has caused my experience of consciousness to burn across my skin like hot sandpaper. Music, long hard walks, and a glass of good wine, can beat it back for a while, but afterwards, the black dog is always there; waiting under a pool of lamplight at the street corner, like a jilted lover.

I'm often asked why I don't take antidepressants, and it's not easy to respond, since the answer is complicated – partly medical but largely philosophical – and crucially linked to being a writer deeply concerned with social justice and the nature of human reality. Depression has three wellsprings: biological, circumstantial and existential. Mine is mostly existential (I've always been appalled by the manifestly unfair way we constitute society) and I think it's important (particularly for a writer) to see the world as it is, not as it might become chemically construed. Despite the occasionally seductive temptation, I wouldn't resort to suicide. Apart from anything else, it's such a fundamentally selfish act, drawing other people, often strangers, into the pain, no matter how hard you might try to isolate it. Years ago, on a long and lonely bushwalk in a West Australian forest, I found the results of a suicide – hose from the car's exhaust neatly taped through a sealed window – and know it's not something I'd wish to visit upon anyone else.

Depression is a black hole that sucks you down into its centre like a drowning whirlpool, where you fear the future, are appalled by the present, and haunted by the past. No matter what you're doing, you constantly feel you should be doing something else, and no matter where you are, you're burdened by a powerful dread that you should actually be somewhere else. Impatience and procrastination drag you in opposite directions, and if all this weren't enough, there's a nagging voice at your elbow, accusing you of letting the side down by not joining in when everyone else is having fun.

Depression has always been a taboo subject. In the middle ages it was known as accidie, the sin of spiritual sloth, and said to 'attack the monk at the fourth hour'. Later it was called melancholia and became a preoccupation of the Victorian poets. In literature it was linked with a crisis of self-confidence; a proposition beautifully explored by William Styron, the author of *Sophie's Choice*, in his fine personal memoir *Darkness Visible*. Writing is a lonely occupation and depression a very lonely illness. Combining the two can produce a monstrous burden, since the pathology of both is linked to consciousness, the greatest unexplained mystery of our human condition.

The human brain is fearfully complex. However, it now seems clear that the biochemistry of a depressed person's brain is different to that of someone who isn't depressed. But which came first – the altered chemistry or the negative perceptive of reality? For some depressives in remission, myself included, there remains an assumption that the black dog – despite its horrifying reality – is simply laying bare an intrinsic truth about society which must be faced sooner or later. And this poses a profound dilemma: If mood-enhancing drugs like Prozac can profoundly alter the way we experience consciousness, how do we sensibly interpret reality? It might be argued, for example, that it is precisely our doubts and fears that humanise and define us, and to get 'well' chemically is to cheat, in much the same way an athlete might take performance enhancing drugs. And what of the notion that likens psychological suffering to an irritant grain of sand producing a pearl? Proust once claimed that nothing worthwhile was ever achieved without neurosis, and Emile Zola, having been examined by a team of psychiatrists, modestly agreed with their findings that his genius was largely the result of ongoing angst.

Spike Milligan's celebrated excursions to his country of a 'thousand grim winters' coincided with some brilliant work, and Winston, at his most Churchillian, was hounded by his black dog.

To be depressed is to be cruelly handicapped. The effects of physical injury can usually be recognised for what they are, and therefore excused or given help as appropriate, but depression tends to be invisible, and therefore prone to serious misinterpretation. It's as if life has been wrenched from you, but somehow you remain alive. As if the vital dynamic of motivation has been surgically removed, like a frontal lobotomy. Yet you remain outwardly unchanged. You get up and try to carry on; you interact with family and friends; you get through the day as best as you can. But then you must face the night again; which is infinitely worse. The hour between three and four in the morning for the clinically depressed is the metaphysical core of loneliness; an isolation so utterly existential it scarifies the soul. Or whatever it is we like to believe is the soul.

'I think, therefore I am,' the seventeenth-century philosopher Rene Descartes famously declared. The addition of a single word registers ownership of my black dog: 'I think, therefore I am depressed.' Of course, I acknowledge that many people can think without getting depressed – clinically, at least, and this certainly doesn't make them lesser beings. Thinking is linked to personality, and I've had to constantly struggle to escape the grotesque reality of a world perpetually crippled by poverty, bigotry and war. For me, living with the black dog is a matter of morality rather than chemistry. I believe depression to be a reasonable response to the often absurd and unfair way we constitute society. When the TV news reader warns me – all too often lately, it seems – that the next story contains images I might find distressing, I can press a button and look elsewhere. Life is not so amenable. As someone who has suffered from depression for much of his life, I've always regarded its origins as existential rather than biological, and this perception further complicates the fragile dynamics of cause and effect.

Our roller coaster ride through the microchip revolution has widened the gap between space-age technology and stone-age human biology to embarrassing, if not dangerous, dimensions. Cyberspace lures us towards a vaporous world of virtual reality, but the flight-or-fight syndrome of our cave-dwelling ancestors hangs around our necks like the ancient mariner's albatross. However, this much is all: we collectively inhabit a speck of cosmic dust in a vast and apparently otherwise unoccupied universe. Surely it is wasteful madness to fatally quarrel over how we choose to live on fragments of that speck of dust? Surely it makes more sense to share what we call life? However we wish to explain it. However we choose to worship it. And ultimately, however we profess to judge it.

Beauty Point (Wallaga Lake), far south coast of NSW
Winter 1999/Summer 2000 (revised 2016)

Essays

Rediscovering Poetry in a Post-Poetic Age

Poetry has always been many things to many people, but an embarrassingly lopsided writer/reader equation has driven it underground: to pub and coffee shop live performance, or the cyberspace shadows of website production and blogs. Paradoxically, back on the surface, in an increasingly crowded, complex and confusing world, there appears to be little trouble filling print anthologies, finding prize money or maintaining a vibrant (if incestuous) Ozlit debate on poetry's definition and purpose. However, an inconvenient truth remains: there are many more people writing poetry than there are reading it, and the sad irony of this Great Poetry Dilemma (GPD) concerns the way insiders probably have themselves to blame, although very few are prepared to acknowledge the possibility.

Maybe it's time we pushed back the furniture, cleared enough space to swing a few theories, and got down and dirty by cutting to the chase. We need poetry in our lives for the same reasons we need music, or the visual arts: to help gather the social and cultural sustenance to nourish a collective imagination capable of carrying us beyond the twenty-first century. But first we must somehow reach a shared understanding about what and where poetry currently is; why it is failing to engage us in the way it once did; and how we might rediscover its curiously redemptive therapy.

Most people can recognise poetry when it is attempted, but few seem able to agree – if contemporary examples are any guide – on what it becomes when it succeeds; although, measuring something as dangerously subjective and seductively affecting as poetry in terms of success or failure is to miss the point. Poetry simply is. Or it isn't. And why it is or isn't has to do with the context and aspiration of those responsible for its creation and existence, many of whom seem to have forgotten that poetry lends itself to celebrating the senses before the cerebellum.

Having tested the basis of poetry's allegedly intrinsic difficulty over many years, and grown increasingly impatient with glib variations of the cop-out response 'If you want to communicate use a telephone' or the disingenuous diversions of so-called 'language' poetry, I'm sufficiently pissed-off to suggest that poetry today is unread because much of it is unreadable. And I'm referring here to more than just a suspiciously arrogant dismissal of meaning – a poet can be forgiven for sometimes hiding in dark corners – it's also the deliberately awkward structures and discordant rhythms that casually jar the eye as well as the ear.

We're drilling near a GPD nerve, so it might be sensible to apply the anaesthesia of some common ground before the pain kicks in. Obviously, good poetry is more concerned with asking questions than finding answers, and inclined to cast a jaundiced eye on the deep and dark stuff that stalks us all. Any aperture focused to this degree of acuity will naturally block light strong enough to supply two-plus-two-equals-four illumination. However, this doesn't mean the reading room should resemble a coal cellar at midnight during a power cut. The remains of a candle can usually be found, tucked away at the back of a cupboard, if you're prepared to look. Sadly, most contemporary poets aren't.

Using metaphor and allusion to turn the screws on language to summon up a sense of that beyond the reach of dictionary definition has poetic validity, pushing a barrow load of arcane bric-a-brac cloaked in wilfully suffocating obscurity doesn't. It merely locks the castle gates with a self-conscious suggestion of teasingly, catch-me-if-you-can cleverness, and seldom rewards the effort of close reading. Frankly, I've always been appalled by the notion of poetry (or any art, for that matter) as a puzzle to be solved, rather than an enriching experience to be enjoyed, and applaud Sam Johnston's robust response: 'Difficult, Sir? I wish it were impossible!' Obscurity makes demands on the reader; clarity makes demands on the writer. Obviously, there's an important distinction to be drawn between clarity and simplicity, but I passionately believe it is possible to be a 'serious' poet and still be understood. It's just a damn sight harder.

Poetry offers a conversation with the imagination of anyone prepared to listen, although this presupposes a level of accessibility acceptable to both sides of the partnership. Of course, one of the chief problems with trying to pin poetry down has to do with its abundantly various forms: from the bush ballad's bouncing banality to the measured discipline of a sonnet, the gnomic economy of haiku, and the tediously ongoing rivalry between free verse and lyric rhyme. Robert Frost once memorably compared writing free verse to playing tennis without a net, and – as a tennis-playing sometime poet – I'm inclined to agree, although I'd have to also confess to dabbling in free verse. Let's face it, who hasn't?

Until quite recently, rhyme was crime, and sniffingly discarded from the Poetry Editor's slush pile, preferably with a pair of surgical tongs. Now, I'm beginning to suspect the postmodernists are hedging their bets by adding a nip of shy rhyme to their sly crime; driven home, as it were, by the eye-opening splash of a toe being dipped into the icy water of comprehension. Heady stuff, since serious poetry (in other words, that likely to be found in little lit mags) was hitherto inclined to fear clarity as politicians fear honesty; which begs Oscar Wilde's quip about intelligibility finding you out.

I grew up in a beautifully rural backwater of 1950s post-World War II England, close to where Tennyson lived and wrote much of his poetry. Not surprisingly, as a child falling rapidly in love with the sounds and patterns of words, I feasted on his lines like a hungry seagull: 'Only reapers, reaping early / In among the bearded barley, / Hear a song that echoes cheerly / From the river winding clearly, / Down to tower'd Camelot'; and many more of similarly mesmerising ilk. I'm certainly not saying all poetry should sound like this – poetry does what it can, in whatever form best suits its mood – I'm merely pointing out that, for most people, this represents ground zero. And we do well to remember that lyric rhyme is easy to do badly but very hard to do well.

Poetry is the mother tongue of language, but requires the kindness of a good teacher to nourish its voice. My primary English teacher wasn't kind; she was a memorably joyless woman of indeterminate age, who one day asked each of my class to choose a poem we enjoyed reading. A week later, we were summoned, one by one, to stand alongside her, at the front of the class, to recite our selections. Most were predictable, having been harvested from the school library children's anthology, but I chose a poem from a battered volume of collected verse found on my father's makeshift shelves. It was Tennyson's heart-wrenching expression of grief: 'Break, break, break, / On thy cold grey stones, O Sea; / And I would that my tongue could utter / The thoughts that arise in me' – but before my faltering tongue could utter much more than the first stanza, I was brought to an abrupt halt by the teacher's imperious command: 'Wait!'

In the awful silence that followed, she turned towards me, her previously weary and long-suffering expression awakening into a frown. 'Why did you choose that poem?'' she asked.

I stared at her in terrified confusion. Because you wanted me to, I might have replied, but could find no words.

'You chose it,' she said, her eyes unblinking, and lips drawn back to reveal an improbable abundance of teeth, 'a few moments ago, at random, because you had forgotten to do as I asked last week. Is that not so?'

I shook my head, managing a barely audible whisper. 'No, Miss.'

She stood up, reaching, with sharp-boned fingers, for one of my ears, and twisting it painfully. 'Then perhaps you'd be good enough to tell the class precisely why you chose it.'

The silence stretched towards infinity, as hot and stifling tears of humiliation stung my eyes. What did I know of metrical beat, strong and steady as a healthy young heart? What did I know of the siren song of cadence? I wasn't even aware of the word. I had chosen that poem because I liked the moody sound of its almost hypnotic rhythm. A simple enough explanation, if only I'd been able to give it voice. But I just stood there, struck dumb by fear in front of my classmates, wishing I was somewhere else. And very soon, I was: bundled into the exile of a draughty corridor, and made to stand alone, reflecting on my unexplained sin, until the morning milk break.

A lifetime later, if I've managed to become any kind of poet, I guess I'm a wild-card player – unheeded as well as unseeded – driven by passion rather than precision; possessing an intuitively tolerable flair for rhyme, and a receptive sensitivity for the Celtic rise and fall of English language cadence, but a dodgy ear when challenged by metric accuracy. In fact, finding a stress-count disparity between tetrameter and pentameter is likely to leave me with a stress-induced headache. Does such academic discomfort necessarily disqualify me? I suspect some of the high-end gatekeepers think it should. But surely emotional honesty and natural cadence are worth as much as any strictly observed metric algorithm? And for an incorrigible romantic, sweating syllable count numbers is apt to feel more like basic bookkeeping than shaping poetry from ancient human tempo.

In my view, a line that looks and sounds temptingly quotable – whatever its syllabic stress structure – is more likely to lure poetry back to mainstream literary status than inaccessibly cryptic allusion, however metrically accurate. The further poetry reaches into its potential audience, the closer it comes to recording 'the still, sad music of humanity' in ways likely to enrich and strengthen our sense of community. The academic purists and heavy breathing postmodernists don't have to close up shop, just ease off for a while, giving something more amenable a chance to seduce us into the forgotten pleasures of reading lines aloud, and perhaps remembering them for longer than a few moments.

We are prisoners of our perception. We see what we expect to see, and often get it crucially wrong. My distantly remembered English teacher lacked the imagination to see beyond her conviction that I had failed (or even worse, ignored) her assignment because she refused to accept that a nervous eleven-year-old boy could have chosen a poem of such adult sophistication for any reason other than a last-minute stab in the dark to avoid being exposed as lazy or forgetful.

The truth was far less contrived, but much more profound: I had chosen that poem because, at a particular time and place, it resonated, emotionally and linguistically, with an intricate web of things, seen dimly before an adolescent dawn, and conjured into being by the less than two percent of our genetic makeup that separates us from the chimpanzee. The cerebral cortex has validated humanity by granting us the extraordinary gift of abstract thought; reflected from fireside stories told in caves, to the fearful wonders of industrial, cultural, political and technological revolutions, and the healing redemptions of love and forgiveness. And all the while, poetry – as a brazenly original and humanising use of language – was part of the amazing journey.

Choosing that long-ago classroom poem has faint but indelible links to the choices we must now make, with our planet slouching towards hell in the hand basket of global warming; pre-emptive war; environmental vandalism; corporate corruption; financial meltdown; and religious, political and racial intolerance. A consummate, chaotic and potentially catastrophic mess caused by the triumph of greed over imagination, and compounded by the emotional and intellectual sterility of a terminally banal popular culture. We need, more than anything else at the moment, a flint to spark some creatively lateral solutions. Poetry can't save the world, but rediscovering its humanity can maybe help us find something that will.

A slightly different version of this essay was first published in *The Australian Literary Review* in February 2010, and later used as a preface for my 2014 poetry collection, *The Shapes of Light*.

Playing with Words

Our world is conjured into being by words. Codified symbols of meaning that belong to us all. Perhaps it's time for us to accept collective responsibility for them before they visit even greater havoc upon us than currently shows up on our nightly TV news broadcasts. Consider, for example, the sinister burden of the words 'ethnic cleansing' or how the iconic power of the word 'freedom' swallows the deceptively dangerous human paradox of wanting government without being governed. Self-interest is a powerful force, but everyone – except absolute cretins – knows that anarchy doesn't work. In the last couple of centuries, the notion of freedom – at a personal as well as national level – has become enshrined in popular mythology. Now it hangs around our necks like the ancient mariner's albatross.

In an increasingly crowded and complex world, freedom is a fatally overworked abstract noun with a suspect credit rating. We simply cannot afford to do and say as we please any more, and in this context, I suggest, political correctness – so easily despised by the free-booting philistine – is little more than a knot in the handkerchief of social conscience, a means of nagging ourselves into behaving decently. We are, as Bertrand Russell once observed, a credulous lot and, lacking good ideas to believe in, we tend to settle for bad ones. (Which might help explain the Hanson phenomenon.) Many people, it would seem, harvest their opinions from the flatulent confidence of John Laws and Alan Jones. Against this alarming scenario, a spoonful of PC seems about as dangerous as an overdose of carrot juice.

Our insufferable species arrogance has encouraged us to take words for granted, to construct reality as if they've always been around. Auden once observed, 'A sentence uttered makes a world appear.' Yes, but for most people it's a world already colonised by language. In the beginning, there were no words. Just a lot of unknown stuff – for want of a nonexistent word – waiting for language to coax it into being. No doubt, a lot more stuff waits in the wings, just beyond our peripheral vision, like shadows on a sunless day. Occasionally, as through a glass darkly, we catch glimpses of these nameless things and are shaken into believing we've had a spiritual experience, or crossed some psychic checkpoint. Reality is more mundane: the paranormal is merely the unexplored normal, and we've simply drawn another line on the map.

Like gods, we play dice with definitions. In a world obsessed with time and money, it's a reductive process. Science and technology push back mystery and superstition, revealing a reality we struggle to express. So we smooth back the edges, prune a couple of thorny bits and squeeze what's left through the template of our perception. By then, of course, it isn't the same thing we started out with but, since everyone is anxious to move on, why waste time worrying about it? The world has long been thus inclined but, with the increasing fragmentation of national self-interest, and a burgeoning fundamentalism, the process has picked up potentially fatal speed. Superficiality is an understandable reaction to a deeply confusing world, but when reality becomes little more than a set of intelligible lies masking unintelligible truths, people like Pauline Hanson are taken seriously, and civilisation – as we have never known it – slips even further from our reach.

Take racism, for example: it's a slippery beast and escapes adequate definition unless pinned down hard and fast. Despite being one of our most enduring and socially destructive evils, it's often misconstrued as little more than an aberration of manners. Slouching towards an Australian republic, we – particularly those who speak and act on our behalf – need to remember that the causes, as well as the effects, of racism must be constantly challenged. In a civilised world, the colour of our skin would carry as much significance as the colour of our eyes or hair, and, although we like to think civilisation already exists, a glance at the evening TV news should be enough to convince us it doesn't.

Sadly, we live in a world where words are used to exploit natural differences in ways which claim to bring us together but actually drive us apart. Take, for example, the so-called battle of the sexes, a seemingly irresistible distraction based on the fatuous notion that men and women are somehow intrinsically different. This urban myth, fuelled by relentless social conditioning and Disneyland pop psychology, uses an obvious – but effectively irrelevant – biological difference to justify simplistic solutions for real or imagined relationship problems. On deeper and more meaningful levels, it merely provides the building blocks of prejudice and inequality. Which happens to be pretty much how racism works.

Our reluctance to find a few words of apology for past and present destruction of indigenous culture, despite being caught red-handed, as it were, is largely due to a lack of will to engage the issue collectively. 'You can't blame me, I wasn't there,' is a specious response, almost like saying, 'I'm not racist, I just don't like blacks.' (Or any other ethnic group you care to mention.) As the poet, John Donne, said long ago, 'Any man's death diminishes me, because I am part of mankind.' Yes, Virginia, confronting racism might be a pain in the arse, but the bell tolls for us all.

The cold reality of a complex society is that anyone with a quick-fix solution hasn't twigged the problem. It's easy to claim to be able to fix something you don't understand. And when people assume they know what's going on, simply because they watch commercial television news or so-called current affairs programs that chase ratings rather than truth, we're in deeper trouble than we might suppose.

Three o'clock in the morning is a dangerous time to think too closely about such things. Some nights I seem trapped inside a metaphysical double loop, as if an invisible hand has scrawled the ABC logo across the bedroom ceiling. One side of the loop goes like this: if the unexamined life really isn't worth living, then how come the bastards doing the least examination seem to have the most fun? And the other side like this: there is no such thing as absolute truth; but if that statement is true, then there is, and if there is, then the statement isn't true. I'm still going round in circles when the dawn chorus begins – thankfully, a song without words.

Sometimes, my insomnia has more to do with a book I'm reviewing, rather than with metaphysics. Perhaps a new novel, not bad enough to be funny in that deliciously unintentional way a truly bad book can be, or good enough, in my opinion, to have been published in the first place. But resting – with a well-known publisher's blessing – in the hands of an Ozlit fringe-dweller with the cheek to question its validity. (Which, for someone as depression-prone as myself, is a pleasant change from questioning my own validity.)

The fact that I've been asked to give an opinion, and am determined to find the words for an honest one, makes me think about the way some reviewers, for reasons of misguided compassion, fear of revenge, or of missing the next literary binge, will fudge responses. In cricketing parlance, they'll let a loose book through to the keeper when it should have been belted over the square leg fence. Which is culpable negligence, since ambitious mediocrity muddies the waters of creative opportunity and cripples literature.

I understand the lonely sweat of creative writing as well as anyone, but the cult of authorship must be resisted. Authorship has to be earned, never assumed. There's a damned sight more to being a writer than simply wanting to be one. Writers have to place higher value on their words and use them with greater economy, care and sensitivity. In this age of advanced literacy, creative writing courses and computer software packages, there are far too many people writing just for the sake of writing: churning out words which lack beauty, grace or ideas, and do very little to help define or enhance the human condition. And let's not inflate literary jargon either: modernism abandons tradition; postmodernism becomes neurotic about it. Full stop!

And consider this proposition for a moment: arguably the most important (and often least considered) factor in the literary equation is the reader, but when you isolate the genuine book-lover from the anxious crowd of wannabe writers, paranoid about who has or hasn't got a grant, or made so-and-so's latest anthology, you tend to find a quiet but determined preference for intelligent, well-written and accessible narrative. Unfortunately, amid the self-absorbed hype and cheap plonk of a postmodernist book launch, people aren't likely to give a stuff about such details.

Playing with words stacks the odds against winning. Answers to the really big questions are probably unknowable. It's a cosmic catch-22: if the fabric of our existence were simple enough for us to understand, we would be too simple to understand it. So we roll the dice and take the highest score. It can be risky. It can also produce original ideas, which, when fluently expressed, become literature. And books are the crowning achievement of humankind. They celebrate the beauty of language and of wisdom. They save us from ourselves.

The Write Stuff

My wife reads Elizabeth Jolley and Catherine Cookson in tandem, believing the printed page to be more about democratic possibility than subjective value judgements. I remember her many years ago on the deck of a freighter in the South China Sea, wearing a bikini and reading Henry Miller's *Tropic of Cancer* while adjudicating a surreal game of mah-jong being played by two of our children. The bikini has long gone, and the children now have families of their own, but her bedside table still displays wonderfully eclectic titles, such as Lawrence Durrell's *Bitter Lemons*, a fat P.D. James crime trilogy and *The Riders* by Tim Winton. She is, I suggest, a writer's reader, and authors should salute her.

I mention this by way of floating the possibility that some readers intuitively resist elitist notions of good writing as a labyrinth which only the cognoscenti can fruitfully explore. Personally, I've long suspected there is far too much talking about writing for its own good. Apart from an unfortunate tendency to celebrate the author as a cult figure, thereby encouraging the wrong people to write for the wrong reasons, such hothouse attentions are likely to make writers too aware of themselves, and good writing – above all else – is simply an unselfconscious expression of original ideas.

It's interesting that there is much less public introspection about the working habits of painters and composers, despite the arguable proposition that the nature of their creativity is at least as mysterious as that of a writer's. In my view, there's not a lot of mystery about the process of writing; it's simply a capacity for taking great pains, combined with clarity of vision. To over-inflate meaning is to encourage interpretations of literature which are morally suspect, intellectually smug and terminally precious.

Serious writing can be accessible without loss of quality. It presupposes an honest transaction between writer and reader, but it can be done.

Oscar Wilde once observed that to be intelligible was to be found out, and there's the rub. We should expose the deliberately arcane notion that writing which is easy to read is, by definition, inferior to that which makes 'demands' on the reader. This arrogant presumption has been around a long time, and occurs in philosophy and science as well as literature. It flows, I believe, from two primary sources. The first is psychological and based on the Emperor's New Clothes Syndrome, since we are all reluctant to admit being confused by ideas others are celebrating as obviously brilliant. The second is metaphysical and concerns the way we see ourselves at the top of the living species hierarchy. After all, what better way to deny mortality and convince ourselves we are indeed something very special than to make our ideas seem impenetrable?

I suspect some writers deliberately seek obscurity in the hope it will be mistaken for quality. I further suspect that it often is.

Clarity, fluency and euphony form the Holy Trinity of writing, and the greatest of these is clarity. Obviously, there's an important difference between clarity and simplicity; I'm talking about making complex ideas more approachable, not reducing them to fatuous levels of superficiality. And we should attack the false assumption that prose which is easy to read must also be easy to write. It isn't. Good prose is easy to read because the writer has worked damned hard to make it so.

Professional writers don't place half-baked ideas on the page in the hope that readers will trawl for hidden pearls. They peel back layers of meaning, like onion skin, until they themselves have a clear understanding of what is being said, and are able to decide if – stripped of superfluity and sugar coating – the idea remains worthy of expression. Since original ideas are harder to come by than most people might suppose, it follows that the honest professional will write less rather than more. A conscious decision not to write is, I suggest, a tragically unrecognised act of courage which deserves our everlasting gratitude. In these dangerous days, when the itch to write threatens to become a public epidemic, perhaps someone should organise a festival to celebrate the process of declining to write a book.

The Sundial

In that other country of the past, where things are done differently, I married an ingenuous girl with smile dimples, big hazel eyes, and hair the colour of a raven's wing. She was trusting and forgiving, and laughed at most of my jokes. We were very young – too young, some people said – and unused to adult ways. Our first weeks of married life had the deliciously innocent flavour of children discovering sin. We laughed a lot and chased each other, leaping over chairs, bouncing off walls and hiding in closets. Eventually, we would collapse onto the bed, tangled like tiger cubs and gasping with laughter until tears filled our eyes. Then, with surprisingly erotic self-consciousness, we would begin to make love. Almost sixty years on, we are still together, although nowadays we are disinclined to leap over chairs.

We were married in a time when most people observed the conventions of courtship and engagement. We met on 26th July 1956, became engaged on 26th July 1957, and were married on 26th July 1958. During our year of courtship before engagement, we discovered some beautifully rambling public gardens. One vague Sunday afternoon, when it seemed as if the entire world had gone somewhere else, leaving us to explore the gardens completely by ourselves, we found a secluded courtyard, protected by formal hedges and flowering shrubs. In the centre was an elegant sundial with a bronze face, Roman numerals and a quotation. Holding hands, our heads touched as we leaned forward together to read the words. From that moment on, the sundial belonged to us and its corner of the gardens became our sacred site. We would visit whenever we could, feeling miffed on the rare occasion someone else had the cheek to show up.

Time and circumstance took us away. Far away. To the other side of Australia, and then to the other side of the world. Always remembering the sundial and imagining it appearing one day in a garden of our own. But, as the years passed and we raised four children, increasingly preoccupied by staying afloat on the white waters of life, the sundial receded into the past, like a half-forgotten dream. From time to time, when browsing in garden nurseries, we would come across one that looked almost like the original, but the words would be wrong. For all I know, our quotation was a sundial cliché, but it seemed to have vanished forever.

Then one day, quite by accident, when helping some friends look for a terracotta pot, we remembered it again. In a crowded corner of the garden nursery, full of gnomes, bird baths and semi-naked nymphs holding water jugs, I glimpsed a section of elegant stone column, topped by a bronze sundial and what appeared to be Roman numerals. Was there anything written on it? And if there was, would it be the right words? These questions pursued me through a terracotta maze of bric-a-brac, until – balanced precariously between a bird bath and a tangle of ferns which seemed to be reaching for me – I was able to make out some words on the sundial's face. But I couldn't read them without standing on the other side, and that seemed impossible without causing mayhem among the water nymphs. I would have to revive a neglected skill, acquired at school while standing in front of a teacher's desk, and refined during the course of a public service career: the useful art of reading an upside-down text. I steadied myself, adjusted my bifocals and read the quotation. It was ours.

My wife had wandered further on and, in an effort to attract her attention without shouting, I fell into the fernery, which appeared to be occupied by a komodo dragon. Clutching a robust water nymph for support, I managed to disguise my stumble as an attempt to read the price tag on the sundial base. I shouldn't have looked. I checked the contents of my wallet, immediately noticing a depressingly large discrepancy, and remembered the parlous state of our credit card. So I brushed myself down as casually as possible, sighed and moved away.

Later that afternoon, having a glass of wine with our youngest daughter, she enquired casually if I had seen anything interesting at the nursery – perhaps a sundial with a particular quotation? Mystified, I turned to my wife, who under cross-examination broke down and confessed. She had mentioned the episode to our family, who revealed the existence of a secret birthday fund. Although my birthday was still some time away, the money could be used now if required. Throwing aside my wine, I dashed back to the nursery, consumed by fears that our sundial had been snapped up by someone with a gold credit card and was being loaded into the cavernous boot of a late-model Mercedes. But, there it was, still surrounded by an army of gnomes and water nymphs.

It's now safely at home in our garden, with its own small courtyard of pebbles, shells and stepping stones. And there's not a gnome or a nymph in sight. You can tell the time with enough accuracy to satisfy most people, except perhaps a garden party of nuclear scientists, and read the quotation without having to look at it upside down. It says, just as it did sixty years ago, 'Be as true to each other as this dial is to the sun.'

The Species That Knew Too Much

Does a tree falling in an empty forest make any noise? Philosophy and science might argue this question, but I happen to know that a tree falling in an empty garden certainly does make a noise. Because I've heard it. Just as Greg Blewett was bowled by McMillan in the second test against South Africa, when conditions were calm in our empty backyard, a large tree came down with a noise like the apocalypse. For the rest of Australia's innings, and sadly for most of Warne's spin-win script, I was busy cleaning up, rendering the area safe and trying to explain to startled birds – appalled at finding their roosting tree demolished after a long day doing whatever birds do – that I wasn't the environmental vandal they were stridently calling me. I'm not sure I convinced them. My wife and I have worked hard over the years to keep the garden attractive to birds, and we wouldn't want it getting around, by word of beak as it were, that our policy had changed.

The tree, incidentally, was a coral. The one with flaming red flowers and thorns. A species known in some circles as the widow-maker, because of its unfortunate tendency to shed major limbs without due care and attention as to who might be passing underneath at the time. They're soft-wooded, look good, live fast and die young, but there was no apparent reason why ours should collapse so completely at the precise moment of Blewett's dismissal. Was he to blame, I wonder? Did an error of judgement, as willow sought leather at the SCG, cause a coral tree to fall in our garden? It's the sort of question that creeps uninvited into my consciousness at three in the morning when the book I'm supposed to be reviewing becomes unforgivably boring and is tossed lightly, or sometimes heavily, aside.

It's not that there are too many books being published simply because too many people are writing them that annoys me most. It's other Ozlit errors and assumptions, such as the absurd notion that obscurity is clever, and the way clarity is scornfully dismissed as simplicity. Or the facile link between runaway sales and success. (A certain hamburger does very well at the cash register, too, but no one would claim it's gourmet food.) Ideas, preferably original ones, should carry a book's success, not the feverish hype of commercial marketing. For real writers, money is far less important than gaining the respect of other writers and, ultimately, the self-respect of being able to face their own work with total honesty.

What does all this have to do with falling trees or cricket, I hear you cry. Not a lot. Except in the metaphysical sense that associations of ideas have, over human history, led us from the slime to the moon. Here, for example, I have used a whimsical coincidence between cricket and a falling tree to make a point about writing, which might lead anywhere, since language defines us as an intelligent species.

Which brings me, by association, to ignorance. Our world is a dangerously complex place, and increasingly, like moths to a flame, we are drawn to the comfort of simplistic solutions. Ignorance is seen as a state of bliss or, as Oscar Wilde's Lady Bracknell charmingly says, 'an exotic fruit; touch it and the bloom is gone'. And yet, if ignorance is the absence of ideas and ideas validate consciousness, then surely ignorance is an absence of life. I remember a schoolteacher from my childhood, not because of his appearance or manner, but through a single, extraordinary act of teaching.

One vague summer afternoon, with most of the class dozing, he drew a white chalk circle on an empty blackboard. 'The inside of that circle,' the teacher said, tossing the chalk from hand to hand, 'represents what we know, while the space outside the circle represents what we don't know.' He paused to see how many of us were listening and threw the piece of chalk with impressive accuracy at one of the more obviously sleeping boys. 'Thus, as our knowledge expands, the rim of the circle touches more of the unknown. In other words, the more we know, the more we realise we don't know.' A complex and abstract proposition, expressed with compelling clarity.

Knowledge is power. It can also be dangerous. In the late twentieth century, humanity's circle of knowledge has inflated like a party balloon on an oxygen cylinder. We've had a ball, and stagger towards the millennium and a thunderous hangover. Because, as the poet said, knowledge comes but wisdom lingers. Technology has made us credulous rather than wise. As truth becomes larger, we become smaller. It's the age of the urban myth and – God help us – of people like Pauline Hanson, whose utterly banal world is so small it would fit inside a pinhead and still leave room for an echo.

Our existence is chaotic. It might also be a huge cathedral of mathematical order. A cathedral so vast we cannot see it all at once. Which is not quite the same thing as saying we cannot understand it. We must strive patiently to reveal further glimpses. By associations of ideas. By chaos theory. And circles.

Does a tree falling in an empty forest make any noise?

A Perception of Eagles

> He watches from his mountain walls,
> And like a thunderbolt he falls.
>
> – Alfred, Lord Tennyson (1809–1892)

A poem of mine contains the lines: An eagle on the updraft from Wallaga's sandy mouth / mocks the law of gravity with breezes from the south.

One evening, not so long ago, burnt out by free-floating anxiety, depression and an increasing sense of global despair, I watch a pair of sea eagles circling lazily in the same place that offered up my poem. Montague Island is a grey shadow on a darkening sea, and the smoothly gliding eagles seem to possess a calmly poetic resonance, steeped in the beauty of its own making. My eyes fill with surprisingly sudden tears, and I glance around, as if embarrassed or ashamed, but the lonely headland embraces only me: a failed humanist, hoping for redemption, and the pair of eagles, magnificent creatures from a different species.

Of course, the eagles are simply hunting for food, but I can't help wondering if my perception of their effortless flight as a metaphor for existential harmony is just a romantic human construct, or something more valuable. Oscar Wilde once remarked that the wrong kind of wallpaper could make him cry faster than a death in the family, and it's easy to slip across the surface of this as an example of intellectually cynical wit, but Oscar was an aesthete, someone who lived for beauty, in much the same way as a drug addict might live for cocaine.

I grew up in a classically beautiful landscape, on the western corner of the Isle of Wight, near the south coast of England, and now, as an adult, well past his biblical use-by date, I sustain my existence by living in a place haunted by echoes of that childhood serenity, near Wallaga Lake, a few kilometres north of Bermagui, on the far south coast of NSW. However, as a writer with a stubbornly lifetime cradled passion for social justice, I'm often paralysed by doubt and can understand something of the idiosyncratic – and possibly dangerous – presumptions of perception. Pre-Christian wisdom summarised the problem well: we don't see things as they are; we see them as we are.

To gain access to the motivation of our own perception is to increase the likelihood of understanding how other people motivate theirs, and regardless of whether we see existence based on faith or reason, achieving a sense of collective meaning is never going to work without first discovering a sense of personal meaning. It isn't just the beauty of the way those eagles defy gravity that makes me weep; it's the terrifying possibility that they are unaware of the joy to be harvested from such an experience.

Arriving home from my walk, I ask my wife if she thinks my eagles draw any sense of pleasure from their effortless flight. Like me, she's a lapsed believer, but quickly replies, 'Of course they do.' I'm not convinced, but hope she's right; because if she isn't, the world would be an even darker place. And that's something I definitely don't wish to know.

The Dangerous Edge of Things

If I had to pick one writer who had most influenced my lifelong love of the way literature can teach us more about ourselves and our world than any academic textbook, the choice would cause some dithering, but eventually settle on Graham Greene. Let me use just one (and perhaps a lesser known one) of his many novels to explain why: consider a journey through post-Franco Spain by a Catholic priest and a recently deposed communist mayor. They stay overnight at a brothel, watch a pornographic movie, start a riot; and all the while never miss a beat of their lively debate on the relative merits of Christianity and communism.

This is the unlikely scenario for Graham Greene's *Monsignor Quixote*, about a recalcitrant parish priest in a small Spanish village who wins an unexpected promotion to Monsignor and takes a motoring holiday with his friend (the recently deposed communist mayor) while his bishop tries to decide what to do with him. Published in 1982, towards the end of Greene's long and busy writer's life, the novel teems with the delicious nuances of irony and morality that haunt the vast body of his work (novels, short stories, essays and plays) that – had it not been for an irksome penchant for getting up the nose of Western imperialism – might have been rewarded with a Nobel Prize for literature.

Graham Greene's depressive temperament involved him with many global trouble spots 'at the dangerous edge of things' in search of escape from boredom and despair. It was a neurotic pilgrimage as well as an astonishing catalogue of creative cause and effect. South America before World War II discovered the whisky priest so vividly portrayed in *The Power and the Glory*; a small cargo ship bound for North Africa, dodging German submarines in 1941, produced *The Ministry of Fear*; a stint with the British Secret Service in Sierra Leone conjured up *The Heart of the Matter*; Vietnam during the last days of the French regime shaped *The Quiet American*; and from the Belgian Congo came *A Burnt*

Out Case. In one of his 'fragments' of autobiography, *Ways of Escape*, Greene confides that

> writing is a form of therapy; sometimes I wonder how all those who do not write, compose or paint can manage to escape the madness, the melancholia, the panic fear which is inherent in the human situation.

In *Monsignor Quixote*, Greene uses his deceptively brilliant talent for dialogue to draw the narrative effortlessly from page to page despite the sophistication of its theme. Here are a couple of examples from the Monsignor on theology and ideology that penetrate the heart of Greeneland:

> '...logical thought does often lead to absurd situations. There is a popular saint in La Mancha who lost her virginity when she was raped by a Moor in her own kitchen when he was unarmed and she had a kitchen knife in her hand.'
>
> 'She wanted to be raped, I suppose.'
>
> 'No, no, her thought was quite logical. Her virginity was less important than the salvation of the Moor. By killing him at that moment she was robbing him of any chance of salvation. An absurd and yet, when one thinks of it, a beautiful story.'

And a few pages earlier, the Monsignor makes this observation to his communist friend:

> 'The proletariat I saw on the Costa Brava were paying for their own holidays. You have to look at the Third World, Sancho, to find any paupers now. But that's not because of the triumph of communism...it was humanism not communism, which turned the pauper into the bourgeois, and behind humanism there's always the shadow of religion...'

Graham Greene died on 3 April 1991, having never entirely abandoned the Catholic Church. His novels remain an important contribution to twentieth-century literature, spanning – in ways few other serious writers could manage – the awkward gap between popular and literary fiction.

Sandcastles

> When I consider thy heavens, the work of thy fingers,
> the moon and the stars, which thou hast ordained;
> what is man, that thou art mindful of him?
>
> – Psalm 8: 3-4, King James Version

There are said to be more stars in the cosmos than there are grains of sand on all the beaches of the world. How anyone could possibly know such a thing boggles the imagination, and to merely contemplate the proposition – standing on the sand near the entrance to Wallaga Lake, on the far south coast of NSW, and gazing northward into salt-misted oblivion along a ten-kilometre beach – is to invite a headache. Followed by a soul-ache (if there is such a thing as a soul and, if there is, assuming it could ache). After a few moments of such contemplation, a huge weight seems to crush everything into dust; or, at least, into a conscious acceptance of human reality as grains of dust on the surface of infinity. For that's all we are, in cosmic terms: a handful of dust, given briefly human shape by words.

I have absolutely no memory of learning to read. Which – given my love of words and the fact that reading has formed such an important part of my life – seems odd. But then, memory – like life – is odd; sometimes very odd. I do remember spending a lot of my English childhood up a tree. I'd often take a book aloft and fashion a sort of nest in which I could lie back and read, pausing every now and then to admire the view. It occurred to me at the time, and occasionally still does – although nowadays I lack the energy, agility or nerve to leave the ground – that seen from a tree, the world seems much improved; and almost believable. Which was important back then, because my lack of belief was even stronger than it is now. Reading gave me something far more valuable than I realised at the time. And even now, despite all the wasteland years of depression and anxiety, it still does: a reason to turn the page on a new day; and the wherewithal to face mortality. Reading should never be taken for granted. The process is elemental to our experience of consciousness. It reminds us who we are.

The trouble with our postmodern life has much to do with it becoming so sophisticated we think we can frame the universe inside a warm laptop. We've lost touch with the natural world in ways important to our sense of wonder. In essence, that's what wrong with poetry and storytelling today: we're so bloody pleased with ourselves; we've forgotten what it means to see the world unencumbered by the barnacles of prejudiced experience, as if for the very first time. Of course, there's a raft of other things wrong as well: such as the way economic rationalism has corrupted the imagination of mainstream publishing; the way a celebrity cult of authorship has encouraged the wrong people to write for the wrong reasons; the way poetry has become so self-indulgent it doesn't even notice its own incoherence; the way an intellectually self-satisfied – and usually self-appointed – cognoscenti has floated literature up a backwater creek, losing the plot as well as the paddle. Yes, all that too, but essentially it's about betraying something deep within ourselves: the honesty, originality and immediacy of an instinctive vision. In short: the child's eye.

Psychology tells us we need to dream. Literature, for similar reasons, tells us we need to read fiction. The word fiction comes from the Latin *fingere*, which started out by meaning to fashion in clay, but evolved into meaning to invent; to imagine, or even to pretend. The English word 'feign' comes from the same Latin root. And it's worth noting that the word 'author' shares its origin with 'argument'. Back in the seventeenth century, Miguel de Cervantes argued his lovably mad knight, Don Quixote, into memorable existence. It's regarded by some as the first novel, although literature had been around for a while. Homer was banned by Plato for telling 'lies' in the Iliad and Odyssey, within whose mythic structure rests the acorn seed of James Joyce's 1922 iconoclastic work *Ulysses*, regarded by many critics as the linchpin of modern literature, despite remaining widely unread. (It's a mistake to tackle *Ulysses* too earnestly. Relax, and try taking turns to read it aloud with someone close.)

Of course, it's easy to forget that the English language was unknown at the time of Christ, and didn't independently exist until the second millennium. Now its almost half a million words – give or take a few thousand – outstrip the range of most other languages, mainly because English has shamelessly taken what it wants, and not been afraid to grow. Arriving in Britain as Germanic seeds from the Angles, Saxons and Jutes, cross-pollinated by Latin and Greek with the advent of Christianity, and fertilised by the Danes and French-speaking Normans, the English language has flowered into a compelling example of linguistic multiculturalism.

When used well, English is such an elegant and graceful language, it seems almost negligent to write anything in a manner that doesn't in some way reflect these qualities; which is partly why I get so upset about the wilful – and often ugly – obscurity of literary postmodernism. My mother, a self-effacing woman of great modesty, who played Scrabble with a quiet dedication to spelling and a stubborn preference for a word whose look or sound would please her, wrote grocery lists, complete with explanatory notes of greater structural beauty, euphony and coherence than some of the so-called poetry I've noticed in recent years. The English language is a magnificent means of communication, and literature can take no plaudits without first acknowledging the extraordinary vigour, resourcefulness and profound beauty of its medium.

I've always been a writer, but despite winning prizes for fiction, non-fiction and criticism, I'm often stifled by self-doubt, and disinclined to sing and dance in the manner required to gain much more than an occasional glance from the selectors. It's a largely self-imposed handicap that can produce a uniquely melancholic taste; a blend of frustration, disappointment and exclusion, all coming together in a spooky recreation of a dreary Sunday afternoon, where nothing much happens – several times.

For me, a lifelong sense of free-floating anxiety, stemming from a negative perception of just about everything, had set in early. In fact, I was little more than a child, and waiting for a bus, when first encountering the awful epiphany of knowing the human condition to be fundamentally unfair, where promises are seldom kept; truth burns you alive; honesty doesn't prevent punishment; deception pays a dividend; heroes have feet of clay; justice is a relative concept and despair a cardinal sin.

The bus, when it eventually arrived, through the frozen light of an English winter, would take me on the first step of a long journey to the other side of the world; to the stark midsummer heat of Fremantle in Western Australia: the promised land of the ten-pound Pom. I now know, like Beckett, that life is defined by waiting: whether for Godot; the kindness of strangers; redemption of a lover; acceptance of an idea; the easing of pain; or ultimately, of course, the oblivion of escape.

I especially remember waiting for the birth of my first child, a daughter, who was named Kerry – by Celtic whim – after a remote region of the west coast of Ireland, which I knew only from stories but regarded as poetic heritage. Kerry was born in a small hospital in the Swan Valley, on the rural fringe of Perth. As my heavily pregnant wife disappeared, together with her pathetically battered suitcase, I was dismissed by a no-nonsense matron as being no longer required. Things were done differently then, and I went quietly, returning to our rented hovel (which is now, I noticed recently, a fashionably terraced and desirable suburban residence) to make myself a consoling cup of tea. And then to wait: through the lonely, restless, and seemingly never-ending night; lamentably uninformed about the reality of birth; and struggling to accept, let alone understand, the nature of fatherhood.

When, next morning, bleary-eyed, and unwashed, I was led into a corridor with a long glass window, behind which stood a row of cots, each containing a raw pink baby, my bewildered gaze could barely focus in the direction of my daughter. Her eyes were closed but she was awake, her miniature hands moving in front of her face, as if already fending off the world. As I watched, spellbound with a complexity of emotion beyond my ability to unravel, I became fascinated by the exquisite but fearful beauty of her tiny fingers, each one tipped by an improbably minute but perfect fingernail. If there is a single aspect of us that captures human fragility more vividly than the hand of a newborn baby then I would like to know what it is.

My wife was good at having babies, and we had three more in quick succession, before making a pragmatic reconciliation with our Catholic faith by deciding on birth control. Unsurprisingly, perhaps, we now have no faith; except in the decency, tolerance and compassion of our four adult children. For us, they are beacons of hope in an increasingly intolerant and dangerous world. Because today, more years after that distantly recalcitrant bus than I care to remember, I am still waiting for all manner of hopeless resolutions, although this time I'm more likely to be doing so with a glass of whiskey close to hand. Irish whiskey, spelt with an 'e', and releasing the mellow sadness of an Atlantic coastline, seen dimly in the Celtic twilight I tried to preserve by naming a daughter after one of its most wild and beautiful regions.

My wife, sensibly perhaps, doesn't drink whiskey (with or without an 'e') but until some years ago, this didn't mean I had to drink it alone, because a dear old friend, Madam Pat Thompson, the amazing jazz chanteuse, even more ancient than me, loved the stuff, despite preferring to drink it with enough ice to offend the meekest Irishman. And so we would sit together, my dear friend and I, in an Australian twilight, to sip our whiskey and consider the bleakness of a contemporary world, with its consummate madness of war; environmental vandalism of insatiable greed; arrogant stupidity of religious and economic fundamentalism; corruption of corporate and political expediency; but also, as the whiskey slipped smoothly across the tongue, the healing redemptions of poetry, music and laughter.

But now my dear friend has gone, and since I am drawn towards shadows rather than sunlight, the odds are weighted against nourishing another whiskey-intimate friendship, leaving me to seek such salvation alone; waiting for answers I increasingly dread to know. For example, over countless millennia the earth and the sun have managed a reasonable homeostasis, which a few centuries of industrial development, culminating in a period of relentless 'economic growth', has tipped towards catastrophe, perhaps irretrievably so. Leaving only a sense of despair at the way recent decades have been wasted by argument and recrimination; by the way global warming has been doubted and denied; how money needed to help find a solution has been thrown at the empty arrogance of weapons and war; and ultimately, by the way we have betrayed our children's heritage. Closing my eyes, the future is hauntingly evoked by an image of my daughter's fingers, shortly after her birth: tiny, fragile and precariously beautiful.

But there's something else – there always is, isn't there? – perhaps even more elemental than creative paralysis caused by despair; something which, thanks to a deeply ingrained work ethic, I'm almost ashamed to admit. It's this: I've always rather enjoyed the aesthetic sense of idleness. The truth is, I happen to like sitting at my desk, staring out through a window, with a nice cup of tea and a cheese and chutney sandwich close to hand, pretending to myself, and anyone else who might ask, that I am working. Perhaps I am, after all, since it might be argued that true writing – as opposed to superficial scribbling – is part of a complex and isolated process that needs a flute of idleness now and then, as the body needs a flask of water. And, anyway, doesn't elemental quietude seem an appropriate response to the noisily chaotic lack of meaning presently driving our mad, bad world, with its posturing arrogance and vacuous morality? A world where prejudice, intolerance and cruelty are fabricated daily in the cause of cultural and economic imperialism. Or gods with as much credibility as Father Christmas.

As a child, the Bible once promised me – poetically, before the awful age of economic rationalism put paid to such profitless pursuits – that things were first seen face to face, but later through a glass darkly. Now, that darkness seduces me into the honey-coated idleness of intensely hopeless reflections, freezing themselves into a mythical landscape, where compassion and justice happily co-exist. Where writers are moved by the passion of having something interesting and original to say, not merely because they've recently completed a creative writing course, retired with a favourable word processing package, or covet the celebrity status of a word festival gig.

Our collective sandcastle of human vanity is in danger of being blown away by the sterile banality of a crass popular culture, contaminated by the self-indulgent ambition of endless economic growth, which, in turn, beckons the doomsday gates of climate change. We choose to live in this dangerously trivialised world, and therefore must share the blame for its most grievous faults; such as the ludicrous paradox of the most powerful nation on earth electing as its leader a man of such blustering bigotry, boastful deception and venal perception as to threaten the survival of us all in a desperately simplistic bid to comfort a deprived underclass. We have all helped to create the shameful existence of Donald Trump; a man, if ever there was one, to truly represent the shabbily withered state of our human condition at the dawn of the third millennium.

We are all responsible for thirty-second news grabs and smart-arsed headlines, where reality is chopped into nibble-sized chunks, selected with prejudice, and firmly gladwrapped against the bacterium of truth; a world where information becomes kaleidoscopic, technique hit or miss and motivation geared to the cash register. A world that provides cosy little glimpses of everything, from tax cheats to test tube babies; terrorists to political spin doctors; sporting heroes to bloated villains; cataclysmic tragedy to game-show greed; and the gross extravagance of rampant materialism to the crystallised obscenity of starving children.

We glance and look away, assuming we know what's going on. We don't. We haven't even scratched the surface! We're breeding a new generation of philistine: shallow-minded, self-interested and fatally disengaged by the vaporous glitter-scope of cyberspace. Is this what we really want? Or truly deserve? Perhaps. Let's pour ourselves a flute of idleness and take a little time to think about it.

Of Chinese Restaurants and Cyberspace

> Conservatives are not necessarily stupid, but most stupid people are conservatives.
>
> – John Stuart Mill (1806–1873)

In those far-off foreign days before digital social media, I fondly remember listening to the BBC World Service when travelling off the beaten track and needing a quick reality fix. The announcers, always male in my memory, spoke in tones cultivated to persuade the Barbarians that God was an Englishman, and that you could believe absolutely everything He said. Hopelessly romantic and probably naive, I was credulously awed by the portentously sonorous introduction: 'Here is the BBC World Service News, and this is London.' There was always a slight pause between the first and second parts of that sentence, with a faint, but recognisable emphasis on the word 'this', as if to suggest that no matter where you were listening, it couldn't, in a thousand years, be anyway near as interesting, or as important, as London.

Nowadays – like many others of my pre-digital generation – I have learned to live with (if not comfortably in) cyberspace, despite being frequently confused, and occasionally intimidated, by computer technology. However, I quickly came to realise that – although they can crunch numbers very fast, providing practically instant access to essential news (such as the latest test cricket scores) – computers don't 'think' like we do. Or arguably as well, particularly where it involves spatial and visual concepts; a proposition validated by the human brain (until recently at least) still being able to match the most powerful computer at chess.

In fact, according to Sandra Aamodt's and Sam Wang's informative briefing on the state of play of neuroscience, *Welcome to Your Brain*, it's time we ditched the metaphor of the brain as a computer, because, as the co-authors charmingly point out (using a metaphor I find irresistible),

> The brain works more like a Chinese restaurant that we know in Manhattan; it's crowded and chaotic, and people are running around to no apparent purpose, but somehow everything gets done in the end – and efficiently too.'

Based on my cautious exposure to the internet, where I'm inclined to be appalled by the sheer weight of its dross, rather than impressed by the extraordinary reach of its sponge-like database, I take comfort in the knowledge that my brain functions more like a Chinese restaurant than a computer. I can certainly respect the intelligence of the people who created cyberspace; it's the intelligence of many of whom sustain its indiscriminately voracious appetite that worries me.

One of life's most tragicomic ironies is how the often astonishingly clever digital revolution appears to have increased the banality and mean-spirited idiocy of routine human interaction, while generating a morally disingenuous social media where truth is trashed, and lies manipulated for personal and political gain. The recent election of Donald Trump is a telling case in point: a man whose deeply flawed character would – by any analysis based on reason rather than fantasy – immediately disqualify him for a leadership role widely assumed to be the most powerful on this planet. As I have said elsewhere, we are all responsible for such a dangerously nonsensical election result, but collective responsibility doesn't necessarily imply collective guilt.

This dizzyingly constant noise of a digital age has allowed the shallow and selfishly opportunistic opinions of people such as Donald Trump to seduce an effectively disenfranchised underclass into believing that complex problems can be solved with simplistic answers. There's a crucial difference between simplicity and clarity that populist right-wing ideology unwittingly overlooks or deliberately ignores. In essence, simplicity reduces everything to its raw elements, thereby choking off linguistic as well as moral dimension, while clarity does its best to express complexity without diminishing meaning, The latter, of course, takes a lot more time and effort, and since human nature tends to seek the quickest and easiest path, like water running downhill, we are frequently lumbered with dangerously simplistic solutions – such as Donald Trump for president of the USA.

'Knowledge comes, but wisdom lingers,' wrote Tennyson long ago, with a quill pen rather than an electronic keyboard; which pretty well sums it up for me. I'm certainly no cyberspace Luddite; in fact, I admire parts of it, and enjoy some, but the abundant growth of knowledge since Tennyson's day has stretched the gap between stone-age biology and space-age technology to a possibly untenable degree, and the effects of this dangerous disparity is disturbingly reflected in the mirror of our psychology. We're clearly a resilient and highly adaptable species, but true intelligence is about putting knowledge to its best possible use, and I suggest the internet is damning evidence of how sadly we have failed this compellingly vital task. Our imagination is a priceless human resource; carbon-free, and arguably never fully tapped. In twenty-first century cyberspace. perhaps we just need to find the right keystrokes to help produce some creatively intelligent results.

The Brer Rabbit Poetry Syndrome

Ben Lerner is a poet, novelist and critic with sufficient literary momentum to get away with such a clever little parlour game as *The Hatred of Poetry* (published recently by the celebrated American House of Farrar, Straus and Giroux). This slim 'monograph' comprising eighty-six pages nods wisely in all the right directions to indulge an academic conceit that might be easily summarised with a single sentence: the reality of poetry will always fall short of the ideal. And while this is most likely true, the deliberately eye-catching and overheated title invites scepticism, if not scorn. I've been around books and writing for more years than I care to remember, and have never heard anyone claiming to hate poetry. There are plenty of people who don't like it, ignore it or find it incomprehensible and irrelevant, but hatred is a far too powerful (and wasteful) emotion to be used in this context; even as a provocative red herring.

The late nineteenth and early twentieth centuries saw many educated Americans embrace poetry with a similar enthusiasm to the way they greeted psychology, perhaps as a plausible attempt to raise the cultural consciousness of a brash new world. There's always been a vaguely precious core to the arts, particularly poetry, which no doubt helped pacify America's early (and largely inchoate) desire for a sense of global gravitas. On a wider canvas, the modernist movement was doing well, including the paradoxically brilliant Ezra Pound, who managed to combine a fatal attraction for Fascism with poetic benefaction for several rising stars, including T.S. Eliot.

The genesis of Ben Lerner's curiously jaundiced take on all this is linked to his admiration for Allen Grossman, an impressively credentialled American poet and critic who died in 2004. Moved by Grossman's 'freakishly brilliant' essays, Lerner reveals the whimsical notion of poetry's 'bitter logic' in preventing its own success ('poetry isn't hard, it's impossible') and other philosophical shavings that sound clever but don't deliver much more than a wry smile: 'Socrates is the wisest of all people because he knows he knows nothing; Plato is a poet who stays closest to Poetry because he refuses all actual poems.'

Lerner's ephemeral sideshow moves into overdrive with his use of the Gothic incompetence of William Topaz McGonagall's poem 'The Tay Bridge Disaster' – 'Beautiful railway bridge of the silv'ry Tay /Alas! I am very sorry to say / That ninety lives have been taken away / On the Sabbath day of 1879 / Which will be remember'd for a very long time' – to illustrate a risibly tenuous suggestion that 'supreme ineptitude' makes a case for the mythical possibility of 'genuine' poetry by producing a negative image. Really? Personally, I wonder if anyone bothered to make sure McGonagall wasn't just having a bit of a laugh at poetry's expense, rather like Ern Malley, minus the talent.

Lerner goes on to consider Keat's 'gorgeous lines of ekphrastic verse' and Emily Dickinson's 'dissonance' and 'famous dashes', before reminding us about Shelley's response to the argument that science had 'rightfully supplanted poetry' by showing how he (Shelley) 'checks the calculative avarice of a materialistic society, offering an alternative to a crass utilitarianism that is blind to everything that can't be instrumentalised; the use of poetry is therefore entwined with its uselessness.' Well, thanks, Ben – that clears things up considerably.

After further musing on the problem of whether writing poetry can be considered 'actual work' (as opposed to what – selling a South American peasant's unplanted coffee beans on the futures market?) Lerner suggests a hatred of poetry might be a way of 'negatively expressing poetry as an ideal'. Gosh! I hadn't thought of that. Just like the old darkroom photographic negative.

Lerner concludes with a few qualifications about how (of course) poetry can offer lots of things to lots of people, before modestly conceding that his theory 'doesn't pretend to be comprehensive'. Indeed.

For me, the most interesting revelation was the technical term for the slash used to separate lines of verse when included in prose being 'virgule', drawn from the Latin virgula – a little rod.

I threw this 'monograph' down, more in frustration than anger, with a growing suspicion that – despite the world weary confidence of its assured academic tone – Ben Lerner's hatred of poetry was little more than a clever, and sometimes witty, allegory; bizarrely akin to Walt Disney's cartoon story about how Brer Rabbit outwitted the cunning Brer Fox by pleading not to be thrown into the briar patch, where, of course, he would be very much at home. All of which is unlikely to shed any new light on the age-old mystery of what poetry is, and why its heartland definition remains so resolutely beyond our reach.

However, frankly, my dear, I do give a damn, and suggest that although poetry today is often unnecessarily obscure, there's a vanishing point of common ground that helps define and celebrate our humanity. And this has more to do with the emotional and intellectual honesty of linking language with imagination to seek empathy, rather than an overheated academy defending form for its own sake. Poetry is the mother tongue of language, and – given a halfway decent chance – can find a voice capable of speaking to us all.

Stories

A Minor Diplomatic Incident

He flinched inside the dream, and came awake, his hand touching the soft, dark silk of her hair. He raised his head from the pillow, listening intently. The sound had been a single gunshot, surely, but was it part of his dream? It was nearly dawn, and already the clammy Asian heat was seeping through wooden shutters that led to a veranda, green with vines and heavy with indolence.

For the past few days, the embassy had been frenzied with diplomatic activity, as reports were made and instructions sought. The crisis had been brewing for some time, and had now completely brushed aside all other topics of conversation on the recent cocktail circuit.

'Why haven't they told us to evacuate the wives and children?' asked Saunders, a young third secretary on his first posting and predisposed to question the wisdom of his masters.

'I suppose they're waiting,' replied a more senior colleague with the right degree of Foreign Service cynicism, 'to see what the Americans will do.'

He slid from the sensuous comfort of the bed and walked, naked, to the shutters. She had not stirred, darkly etched against the white sheets, her breasts exposed and lips slightly parted. He leant closer to the shutters, squinting through the strengthening light in the direction of the village. Nothing moved.

The ambassador reached for a folder marked secret, and shifted uncomfortably in his chair at the head of the conference table. 'At the moment, the government appears strong with senior army figures giving support.'

He paused to glance down the polished table, noticing the curious beauty of its dull glow in the soft florescent light weeping from the sound-proofed walls and ceiling. The senior and middle-ranking embassy officers sitting in their customary weekly conference positions, waited patiently for the ambassador to continue.

'However, we have been warned to expect the unexpected.' A faint smile touched the corners of his mouth, and he briefly scanned the watching faces, as if to see the effect of the cliché. 'We've received no instructions regarding evacuation of our families, although the embassy in Bangkok has been asked to have reception facilities prepared.' He looked up from the folder.

The first secretary, a man of cool intelligence, whom he liked socially and respected professionally, was writing something on a small notepad. Barlow, ostensibly the information attaché but actually the security intelligence representative, was reading from a recently decoded telegram, while the commercial counsellor was looking bored.

The ambassador, an old-school diplomat, frowned and continued. 'I have an appointment to see the foreign minister this afternoon, and hope that by this evening we should have a somewhat more clear view of the situation.'

He stared through the shutters at the village, now bathed in liquid light. Apart from a few scrawny chickens scratching in the dust, nothing moved. A chorus of chirruping and clicking swelled as birds and insects greeted another steamy day, and sleeping dogs were shaking and scratching themselves into dreary wakefulness. For some unknown reason of instinct, he stared harder at the village, an untidy cluster of rotting timber, rusting corrugated iron and straw roofs. Nestled in its lush green fold of the surrounding jungle, it looked ugly and incongruous; like a scar on the face of a beautiful woman.

The first secretary picked up the phone with irritation, his mouth still working on the after-dinner mint.

The ambassador's voice came crisply on the line. 'Sorry to disturb you, Tony, but we need to speak at the residence immediately.'

The ambassador was alone in his study when the first secretary was ushered in by a houseboy dressed in a white jacket and black trousers. The ambassador's face was set hard as he waved vaguely in the direction of a chair and handed over a single sheet of paper that carried the words 'Immediate' and 'Secret' stamped in red at the top and bottom of the page.

It seemed the situation had deteriorated rapidly. The Americans were making arrangements to airlift all dependants and non-essential personnel to safety, and the ambassador had received instructions to follow suit. To facilitate this, a specially chartered aircraft would be arriving early the next morning.

The ambassador spoke carefully. 'Tony, I want you to contact everyone. There is to be no panic, but they must be at the airport tomorrow morning ready for departure at 0600 hours.' In matters of importance and precision, the ambassador liked to use the twenty-four-hour clock. 'They are to carry the absolute minimum of luggage, and to avoid talk with locally engaged staff – is that understood? Myself, you and Barlow will remain behind for the time being.'

The ambassador returned his attention to papers on his desk, and seemed to have dismissed the first secretary, but then remembered something. 'Oh, Tony, I had a call from Barlow just before you arrived. Some damn nonsense about the police picking up young Clifford's car in the restricted area of Sahur Province. It's probably a mix-up, but see if you can make sense of it, will you?'

He pushed the shutters slightly open to get a better view. Something was wrong. The village was too quiet. By this time there should have been children playing on the dusty track, and women fetching water. There was no sign of life at all. No smoke from cooking fires, no sounds of a village awakening. Nothing. Just a sinister and increasingly threatening silence.

The first secretary held his hands over his ears as the scream from the massive engines increased, whipping sand and debris across the tarmac as the huge plane taxied into position. Although it was only ten to six in the morning, the heat had already softened bitumen beneath the forlorn pile of suitcases stacked alongside the cargo hold. As the pilot cut the engines, the first secretary heard Barlow shouting unnecessarily into his ear.

'Any news of that fool Clifford?'

'Not a bloody thing – his houseboy said he's been gone since yesterday afternoon.'

Barlow gave a crooked smile. 'I suppose you know he's been screwing a native girl?'

The first secretary frowned and looked away, noticing the ambassador hurrying towards them. 'The plane will be ready to leave in twenty minutes, sir.' As the first secretary spoke, he saw tension in the ambassador's face.

'Thank you, Tony. Please make sure everyone boards promptly. Have you heard from Clifford?'

The first secretary was about to reply, but Barlow got in first. 'The region where he was last seen is in an extremely difficult area. It's been impossible to get any information out of there since midnight.'

The ambassador regarded Barlow coldly. 'The chief of police is waiting for me in the airport lounge. I shall have to let him know one of our junior officers is missing.' And with a brief nod to the first secretary, the ambassador abruptly moved away towards the main airport building.

The girl was still asleep. The sun had cleared the top of low hills on the far side of the village, and light was streaming in through the shutters, slicing through the gloom like golden knife blades. The first bullet struck him just above the jaw and smashed on into the back of his throat, stifling the scream that welled in his lungs as the second and third bullets ripped into his chest. As he staggered back across the room, he caught a fleeting glimpse of hundreds of jungle birds taking to the air in fright, and with his young life ebbing away, he heard the muffled thumping of their wings, becoming ever softer, carrying him to infinity.

The ambassador rejoined the first secretary and Barlow as the plane lumbered off down the runway and dragged itself into a metallic sky. The ambassador's expression was grim. 'There have been reports of heavy fighting in Sahur Province.' He took a deep breath. 'The area where Clifford's car was found has been taken over by the insurgents.'

'Christ!' muttered Barlow. 'How the fuck are we going to explain that?'

The ambassador's shoulders stiffened. 'I'm fully aware of the possible political consequences. I want to see you both at the residence right away – and Tony, you'd better pick up Clifford's file from the embassy on the way.'

The room was in full sunlight now, the shutters having been torn open by savage entry. Clifford's body lap crumpled at the end of the bed, his eyes open and staring, but already covered by an opaque glaze, as if they were looking inwards. The girl was no longer beautiful. Her naked body had borne the rage of brutal and merciless revenge. Only the face remained untouched, and it was turned towards Clifford, with eyes, not yet glazed by death, but darkened by a dreadful sense of loss.

The first secretary took another mouthful of the ambassador's duty-free scotch and slumped further into the chair as relaxing warmth spread through his body. The ambasador was at his study desk, reading Clifford's file while the first secretary and Barlow sat waiting with glasses and the whisky bottle on a small table between them.

After a while, the ambassador spoke quietly, as if thinking aloud. 'He was active in politics at university. Only been with us a year – first posting, age twenty-four, good sportsman, with excellent career prospects.' He paused, replacing the file on his desk, next to the police report describing how Clifford's body had been found in the village. 'Do either of you suppose there's any truth to this claim that he was assisting the insurgents?'

The first secretary glanced at Barlow and leant forward, his voice clear but tense. 'Clifford was idealistic. Look at the way he worked himself to exhaustion last month helping villagers in Sahur during the floods. But I totally reject the notion that he would jeopardise a promising career to further some obscure political motive.'

Barlow helped himself to a large nip of the ambassador's whisky, and said expansively, as though it were the only possible explanation. 'I think you'll find it's much simpler. Young lad like that, first time in the tropics…'

The first secretary glanced across sharply. He had the awful feeling that Barlow was going to wink, but mercifully he didn't. He just pushed on.

'And some of those native girls can be…very persuasive.'

This time, both the ambassador and the first secretary gave Barlow a close look, but he was staring at his whisky, as if in reflective consideration.

'Could happen to anyone. The important thing is to play it down as much as possible. Very low-key – you know…' He looked up, pausing before delivering the verdict: 'A minor diplomatic incident.'

This story was first published almost forty years ago, in *The Canberra Times*.

Conversations with a Friend

> The fascination of what's difficult
> has dried the sap out of my veins,
> and rent spontaneous joy and natural
> content out of my heart.
>
> – William Butler Yeats (1865–1939)

Her eyes are lazy with recrimination as she touches my hand. 'Sometimes the people who shout loudest about freedom are the ones most likely to deny it to others.' She pauses and looks away, as if embarrassed. 'Anyway, the world can't afford freedom any more. It's not freedom we should be shouting about, it's decency, tolerance and justice.' She meets my eyes and holds the gaze too long. 'But to answer your question, I'd say your imperatives were those of a politician.'

I raise a hand in protest. 'I'd hoped they were those of a poet.'

'Define poetry,' she challenges.

'Truth on fire.'

'Define truth.'

'Subjective illusion.'

'I don't follow. Redefine truth.'

I glance at the dimly lit restaurant. 'The difference between appearance and reality?'

'Define reality.'

I reach for the long fingers, pressing them gently against the table. Stopping the restless beat. 'Right now,' I whisper, 'this precise instant.'

She hesitates, then pulls away. Toying with the knife on her discarded plate. 'It's gone.'

'What has?'

'The instant.'

I pause; weighing the options. 'That's the trouble with reality. It never stands still long enough to allow definition.'

She glances up, the dark curls flying, and I remember the satin glow of her naked flesh. The fingernails gleam redly as she taps the tablecloth. 'I would have defined reality as politics.'

I watch her in the candlelight. 'That's good.'

'Is it? Didn't you tell me that everything is, in some way, political?'

'Did I? I may have done.'

'It would make politicians more interesting.'

'Perhaps.' I want to change the subject, but her eyes won't let me. 'More relevant, at least. How would you define a politician?

'That's easy. A good one – and they're rare, but not as rare as most people suppose – is someone who knows how to balance the pessimism of the intellect with the optimism of the instinct.'

Surely I hadn't told her that as well? I smile. 'For one awful moment I thought you were going to say balance the books. What about a bad politician?'

Her head tilts to one side. 'That's even easier. A bad politician is someone who lets self-interest get too far ahead of community interest.'

No, I certainly hadn't told her that. I twist my napkin into a rope and push it onto the table. 'Personally, I find politicians, good or bad, pathologically boring.'

'That's unworthy of you,' she chides softly, as the waiter arrives with coffee, cheese and liqueurs. 'Boredom is a kind of death.' She takes something from her bag, passes a hand across her mouth and reaches for a glass of water.

'What was that?'

'What?'

'The tablet?'

She hesitates, as if measuring a secret. 'It was nothing. Just an antidepressant.'

Shocked, I meet her eyes. 'I had no idea…'

'Didn't you? Don't worry. The real thing can be hard to pick sometimes. Even by the experts.'

I remain silent and she adds softly, 'It's nothing to do with us.'

'What is it to do with, then?'

She shrugs and leans back. 'Oh, life, I guess. It can look pretty bleak when you're alone at three o'clock in the morning. Rather like staring into a cesspit full of death adders.'

The image, so casually drawn, strikes me across the face like an open palm. 'But…why?'

She pauses to allow a slow smile. 'When you watch the things on the evening news, you begin to suspect that anyone who isn't on antidepressants ought to be bloody well ashamed of themselves.'

'What sort of things?'

She gestures vaguely with upturned palms. 'Belfast, Belgrade, Jerusalem. Rainforest degradation, AIDS, ozone layer depletion. Indigenous land rights. Random massacres with automatic weapons. Corporate selfishness. Economic rationalism. How's that for starters?' She looks closely at me for a moment, as if unconvinced that I am listening. 'And the stupid, pathetic little people who think owning a gun has something to do with freedom.'

I look away. 'I didn't know.'

'About what? Guns and freedom?'

'No, for Christ's sake! The depression.'

'Oh, that.' She meets my eyes again. 'It's a taboo subject, that's why. But don't worry. The fact that I take a tablet after dinner is really not important.'

'Of course it's bloody important. Depression bad enough to warrant medication has to be important.'

'Does it?' She is looking down at her hands, and glances up without moving her head, the hazel, wide-apart eyes fringed by black, curling lashes. 'Why?'

'Because I care about you.'

Her face seems to freeze, then tug itself downwards, the lips quivering. 'No you don't. Not really. Not in a way that matters.' She pulls a tissue from her handbag and dabs her face, crying softly, like somebody whispering a hushed and private prayer.

I reach for her clumsily, but she pulls away.

'People take everything for granted nowadays.' Her voice is low but urgent. 'Nobody cares about anything in ways that really matter. And that's the entire fucking point, isn't it?'

I've never heard her use that word before. The impact is awful. And its resonance goes on and on, ringing into silence. The way the sound of shattered glass seems to dwell beyond the moment. Long after the last tiny splinter has come to rest…

…an old man is playing chess with a truck driver.

'Come on, grandad,' says the younger man, winking at the barmaid, who has paused, expressionless, to watch for a few empty moments. 'Ya thought I'd be a pushover, didn't ya? Didn't think I was a real chess player.'

The old man continues to stare at the board. 'You're not. A real chess player knows the game is greater than the result.'

I turn away, back to the bar, and a heavy face, coarsened by stubble and increasing rage, fills my vision.

'It's a bastard waiting for them bastards to stop carrying on like a pack of ignorant bastards.' He drains his schooner while I try to penetrate the statement. But he hasn't finished. 'It's fucken different out here, you know. A man needs a gun for all sorts of reasons. I love me rifle. I keep it clean. It shines like a fucken gem. Had it for years. Since I wasn't much more than a kid. And I wouldn't shoot anyone.' He considers this. 'Except maybe some city bastard who comes out here to take it off me.'

I clear my throat. 'If you've had it that long, it's not likely to be the sort of gun they're talking about. You see, there are some things so important we need the same laws for them right across the country. That's what the debate is really about.'

'Debate?' He manages to make the word sound obscene. 'Them bastards could debate all bloody week and still not agree what day it was.' He fondles his empty beer glass reflectively. 'What they need is a bloody good kick up the arse to remind them where the real world is.'

'Where is it?' I ask foolishly.

He peers at me with renewed suspicion, then bellows over my shoulder. 'Maisie, love. Another schooner down here, please. Me throat's as dry as a bunyip's bum.' He winks at someone behind me and then, lowering his massive face back to mine, adds, 'Who did you say you were, mate? You're not collecting for one of them new-bloody-fangled religions, are ya?'

I glance down the bar at Maisie. She has lost interest in the chess players and is filing her nails, pretending to examine them critically. Eventually she gives a soft, resigned pout and saunters towards us, hips sliding from side to side, face frozen with cosmetics and boredom. She shoots me a look of insolent sexuality as she pulls the beer. And the honey-coloured liquid foams upwards as I turn for the door…

…the bush ticks with heat and secrets.

'The country's gone to the pack,' he says.

I lean against the warm tractor. 'What went wrong?'

He spits into the dust. 'Too much assistance and not enough help.'

I'm looking across a flat, brown landscape into a washed-out sky. 'You think a change of government will make any difference?'

His face twists, as if he has swallowed something sour. 'Like the man said, no matter who you vote for, a fucken politician always gets in.' He scratches his groin thoughtfully. 'Bugger this for a joke. I'm taking Mum and the kids back to the city. Get a nice triple-fronted brick veneer somewhere near the beach.' He kicks a tyre as if it were alive. 'There's bugger all left out here.'

'What will you do in the city?'

'Dunno. I'll have a bit left over to invest, I suppose.' He glances sideways and grins. 'And there's always the dole. I paid me fucken taxes.'

A swirl of dust ripples the weeds near his custom-made leather boots…

…a steady throb of machinery echoes from the cathedral roof of the huge workshop.

'You can't trust anyone nowadays,' he says conversationally.

'Why not?' I ask.

'Trust doesn't exist like it used to. Everyone's got an angle.'

'Compromise can be a basis for trust.'

'But then you're stuck with the chicken and the egg problem: what comes first? My compromise or yours?'

'But surely if people were prepared to talk to each other – '

I'm stopped by a snort of pain, and assume the lathe has taken one of his fingers, but he switches the machine off and I realise the cry was derision.

'Talk, talk, bloody talk.' He wipes his hands on a filthy rag, pushes up the safety goggles and reaches into his overalls for a cigarette. 'You could try amalgamating some of the union reps and put a few of 'em in parliament. You know, half on the government side and half on the opposition.' He gives a sly grin. 'That might help.'

'Interesting idea,' I reply, trying to decide if he is being serious or sending me up. 'What about party lines?'

This is met by another snort. 'Bloody party lines!' He stabs a finger in my face. 'You know what's wrong with this bloody country?'

Dirty fingernails, I wonder, shaking my head.

'Bloody party lines,' he sneers. 'Too many bastards worrying about what the party needs and not what the country needs.'

'Which is?'

He takes a long drag on his cigarette and I notice the huge No Smoking sign above his head. 'A bloody good kick up the arse.'

'Why don't you consider doing that, then?'

'Me?' He sounds surprised. 'It's got fuck-all to do with me, mate. I'm going bush. Get back to basics. Got me eye on a nice little place that'll give the wife and kids a bit of fresh air and room to move.' He begins to adjust the lathe. 'It's a bloody rat race in the city, mate.' He crushes the cigarette under a heel and pulls the goggles back over his eyes. He grins and gives me the thumbs up sign.

And I remember a schoolboy comic hero, Biggles…

…a rosy, almost religious, light seeps through the motel room as the neon sign outside the window beckons the travel weary.

Sleepless in the lonely bed, I switch on the television. Talking heads with a moderator struggling to regain control.

'– the key is credibility now –'

'– are you calling me a liar –'

'– truth is rarely absolute –'

'– definitely for your lot –'

'– particularly with your –'

'– gentlemen, please can –'

'– I'm not going to let –'

'– he called me a liar –'

'– you bend the truth –'

'– morality is kept –'

'– but not for you –'

'– what does your –'

'– everything we –'

'– nothing more –'

'– credibility –'

'– ridiculous –'

'– gibberish –'

'– twaddle –'

'– absurd –'

'– idiot –'

'– but –'

I stab the off button and the words tumble into silence. Turning my face to the wall, I watch the shadows flicker on and off, thrown by the rosy light entering the room. Without invitation; like the stutter of unwanted memories…

The candle flame shivers as the waiter serves more coffee, and she crushes the tissue into her handbag.

'You were away for almost a week.'

I nod. 'Had no choice, I'm afraid.'

'Why didn't you tell me you were going?'

'I'm sorry. I didn't realise you needed to be told.'

She looks down at her hands again. 'There's something else I should have mentioned about politicians just now.'

'What?'

'They never seem to understand what's really important.'

I raise a hand for the bill, knowing it was over but feeling no pain. Not yet. That comes later. It always does. Pain validates life. Like the way tram conductors used to punch a hole through your ticket, nod and move on. Satisfied you've paid enough for the journey. So you stare out the window and try to forget what you don't need to remember. It's never easy. Particularly for people like her. The ones with the fascination for what's difficult. For the questions that have no answers. For them, an abrupt ending is usually for the best. It's a clean wound that heals with time. That's what really matters, isn't it? And anyway, I'd just held my seat against the odds, but now it was marginal. Too marginal for her.

The Frozen Sea

Dedicated to the memory of Randolph Stow

The trouble with writing in this country, I thought, boarding the long, sleek train in Sydney for its three-day cross-country pilgrimage, is a lack of literary conviction in the cultural anxieties of a post 9/11 global reality. And this, together with poetry's declining relevance, has gathered enough self-indulgently wilful obscurity to muddy the waters of mediocrity, and seduce people who should have known better into assuming the higher ground belonged exclusively to them.

Having just returned from lengthy exile, and wanting to regain a lost sense of the landscape, I'd rejected the anonymous jet hop in favour of a time-consuming, but geographically intimate, rail journey. I settled into my small but comfortable first-class cabin, with its fold-down bed and fold-up loo, and watched the final flurry of farewells on the platform. As we snaked through the vaguely depressing inner suburbs, I glanced again at the 'little' Australian literary magazine that had prompted my jaundiced observation of a few moments earlier. The stories were so brittle and self-consciously clever, the poems intense and coyly inaccessible, and essays precious with the inflated gravity of straining to impress peer group intellect and frighten any lesser beings found wandering too close to a forbidden sun.

I threw the magazine down and returned my gaze to the dreary urban scene, spooling past my window like a roll of grainy film. There's something about train travel that lends itself to melancholic contemplation. Perhaps it's the gentle speed of passage, framing landscape and thought with remembered empathy. We're all in such a bloody hurry nowadays, with our laptops, iPads (and Pods) and ubiquitous cell phones, the relentlessly increased pace may have disturbed some elemental rhythm.

I'd spent the past decade teaching Australian literature at a minor university in rural England, where the seductions of springtime daffodils and gloomily wooded dales had helped my stealthily declining professional ambition to fatally wither a shaky marriage and send me in search of a much-needed sabbatical to the sleepy south-west coast of my West Australian childhood. During the long flight from London to Sydney, I'd reread, with great enjoyment, Randolph Stow's novel *To the Islands*, and been seduced by the sensitivity and skill of the way he created Heriot, his life-damaged central character, validating a mystical presence for place, purpose and silence. And now, although staunchly denying any middle-aged crisis, I was beginning to suspect myself of being Heriot's fellow traveller on his final flight for lonely redemption.

After dinner I sought distraction in the lounge car, taking a book of Stow's poetry, into which I intended to retreat at the first hint of intrusion. Travel, I told myself darkly, breeds a synthetic camaraderie that quickly evaporates at journey's end. In such a mood, I glanced anxiously at the old man settling into the seat next to me. He was thin and bony, with long white hair falling over a world weary and defeated face. But his eyes – a deep-set grey – were intelligent, and watchfully alive.

'It's not often you see people reading poetry these days,' he said.

He'd caught me by surprise, and I made the fundamental mistake of meeting his gaze with a smile. 'Maybe that could help explain why we're in so much trouble.'

He glanced away, as if finding the attempted joke offensive. 'Did you know the title of that collection, *A Counterfeit Silence*, was suggested by Thornton Wilder's novel *The Bridge of San Luis Rey*?'

Christ, I thought, I've been ambushed by the only person on this bloody train who still reads poetry. I shook my head, making a mental note to find a book on stamp collecting for future solitary travel.

'Yes,' the old man continued, settling down in his seat, and fixing me with a steady gaze again. 'Manuel and Estaban had gone to the theatre for the first time and hadn't understood a word of it.' He crossed his legs comfortably. 'Wilder's point was that speech for them was a debased form of silence, and poetry a debased form of speech.'

I stared at him, like a kangaroo caught in the shooter's spotlight, and longed for silence of any kind.

As if reading my thoughts, he leaned closer and said softly, 'And if they should ever tempt me to speak again, I shall smile, and refrain.' It sounded like a quote, and as I hesitated, he reached over and tapped the cover of my book. 'It's in there. Perhaps you haven't come across the line yet?'

I began to feel hot and uncomfortable, but was unexpectedly rescued by a big, athletic fellow I'd noticed earlier, being farewelled on the platform by a tired-looking woman and two young children.

'G'day,' he said cheerfully, staring straight at me and ignoring the old man. 'I'm Jim Brown. You going right through to Perth?' I nodded as his face disappeared behind a huge fist clutching a can of beer. 'Top spot, the old Perth,' he said, wiping his mouth with the back of his hand. 'Best-looking women in Australia.'

I met his eyes. 'Was that your family back there on the platform?'

His face hardened and he glanced down at the book on my lap. 'Whatcha reading?'

'Poetry.'

'You mean Banjo Paterson stuff?'

'Not exactly,' I mumbled, slipping from my seat and smoothly past him.

At the lounge car door, I glanced back. Jim Brown had taken my place beside the old man and seemed to be giving him a lecture. I turned towards the rattling sanctuary of the carriage link with a sense of timely escape.

Next morning, on the way to breakfast, I was joined by the old man, and it seemed churlish to ignore him, so I mentioned my pleasure in rereading *To the Islands*, and we talked pleasantly about literature and travel, without exchanging names or any personal detail, meeting up again after lunch to settle in a quiet corner of the lounge car with a couple of beers. The train had crossed the mountains and was heading for the drier colours of an interior landscape.

I noticed Jim Brown at the bar, chatting to a young woman, and said, 'There's the Man from Snowy River.'

The old man followed the direction of my eyes. 'Oh, he's harmless,' he replied, making it sound as if I considered Jim Brown a threat.

'I've been overseas for a long time. Surely we're not still like that?'

Surprisingly, the old man became defensive. 'He's not so bad. He was telling me about his family last night.'

'I saw them waving goodbye in Sydney. He doesn't seem to miss them.'

'Don't waste time on him,' the old man replied. 'Tell me what you made of our friend, Heriot.'

The question startled me for a moment, then I realised he was referring to the central character in Stow's novel, *To the Islands*, and I hesitated, suddenly fearful.

He seemed to read my hesitation. 'You thought Heriot was afraid?

I gave a slight nod. 'Aren't we all?'

'Of death? Oh, the means, perhaps, but not necessarily the event.'

We sat in silence for a moment.

Jesus! I'd taught people how to read stuff like this. I took a deep breath. 'He ran away. I know he thought he'd killed someone, but why didn't he stay at the mission and sort it out?'

'You have no sympathy for him?'

'Yes, of course. But he wasn't he a trifle…paranoid?'

'Can you think of him as Everyman?

I sipped my beer. 'Maybe.'

He gave a tiny smile. 'King Lear?'

'I may have neglected my Shakespeare.'

'A Christ figure, then?'

I forced a smile. 'That might be straining the metaphor.'

He was relentless. 'A symbol of the modern Christian dilemma?'

I shrugged. 'I'm not sure I'm interested in the modern Christian dilemma.' Sensing his disappointment, I immediately felt sorry for him and added gently, 'Don't you think it's possible you might be over-playing Heriot?'

He glanced towards the bar, where Jim Brown was still talking to the young woman. 'Perhaps I am. After all, he's merely a character from fiction.' He turned back to meet my eyes, and a curious stillness held his gaze. 'Is he not?'

'Heriot,' I said eventually, struggling to remember some critical theory, 'was trying to give his death a sense of tribal meaning.'

The old man surprised me by smiling. 'Do you suppose Mr Brown is trying to give his life a sense of tribal meaning?'

That night, sleepless on my bunk, I reread passages from *To the Islands*, searching for something I might have missed that could explain the old man's obsession, and was drawn again and again to Heriot's achingly dying words as he scans the empty sea for his invisible islands. My soul, he whispers, against the sound of breaking waves, is a strange country.

At breakfast, Jim Brown loomed massively between us as he leant over our table. 'You two bastards still talking poetry?'

I looked up. 'What's wrong with poetry?'

The friendly grin widened. 'I didn't say there was anything wrong with it, mate. Providing it's used in the right place.'

'And where, Mr Brown,' the old man asked, 'might that be?'

Brown rubbed his unshaven chin. 'I dunno, Prof. Poetry's poetry ain't it? I mean, it might help get your girlfriend into bed, but I can't see that it's a right and proper subject for two grown men to talk about all the time.' He straightened and winked. 'People might think you're just a pair of old poofters.' He jabbed me on the shoulder. 'No offence, mate.' He turned and moved away, chanting under his breath, 'There was movement at the station, for the word had got around…'

Reaching for my coffee cup, I swore softly, and looked up, surprised to find the old man watching me calmly.

'Remember,' he said, 'I shall smile, and refrain.'

We talked a lot after that. Not always about Heriot, but about ideas, places and events. Curiously, we never exchanged personal information, other than first names, as if there was some unspoken agreement, based on the knowledge that as soon as we got to Perth we would go different ways, and such detail would introduce a formality that might disturb the balance of our instinctively tuned dialogue. He was obviously intelligent and well-read, and I was tempted more than once to ask a personal question, but his cool, grey eyes seemed to read this inclination and wordlessly bind us to our contract of silence.

'Randolph Stow,' I said, trying to make up ground, as we lingered in the lounge car on our last night with a couple of whiskies, 'was concerned with man's place in society, and the alienating effects of imagination and spiritual identity.'

'And what was Heriot's spiritual identity?'

I glanced towards the darkened window. The desert? I thought, but said nothing. Tomorrow we arrived in Perth, but I felt as if I'd been swallowed by the unforgiving silence of the Nullarbor.

The old man placed his empty glass on the table between us and tapped its rim with a fingernail. 'This is held together by millions of tiny heat-blasted grains of sand. Individually, they're useless dust. But together, they form a circle of strength and beauty that gives meaning and purpose to their existence.' He paused. 'Do you remember the final scene where Heriot is staring into the sun from his cave in the cliff?'

A blade of fear touched my face. 'I remember.'

'And how he made one last attempt to change the world by throwing that stone down into the sea?'

I nodded, unable to speak.

'But, of course, the world remained unchanged.' My companion paused. 'Heriot's stone disappeared into a sea that will always be unreachable.' He met my gaze and a tiny bubble of stillness seemed to bond us with the depth of universal poetry. Then he glanced down at his empty whisky glass. 'Heriot was trapped inside the truth of his existence just as the grains of sand in this glass are trapped in theirs.' He turned his head towards the darkened window. 'We are all prisoners.'

I made no reply, and he stood up. 'Tomorrow morning our journey together is over.' He held out a hand. 'I've enjoyed our little talks. Thank you. Good luck and goodbye.'

I struggled to my feet and took the outstretched hand; its grip was firm, cool and dry, like a page from an old book.

'But surely we'll see each other again?'

'I think not,' he said, and paused for a moment, as if uncertain whether to share a secret. 'Didn't Kafka say something about how books can break the frozen sea within us? Stories and poems are powerful, but they alone can't change the world. They can, however, change the way we see the world, however marginally. And that must be a good thing, because the process is humanising.' The old man paused again, before adding softly, 'And humanity can save us from ourselves.' Then he turned away before I could reply.

I ordered another whisky and sat alone, nursing it for a while. The lounge car was empty, as passengers prepared themselves in their cabins for morning arrival. I glanced back at the table as I left. The two whisky glasses were standing in their shared circle of light, like lonely beacons from a place already beyond my reach.

As the train rattled down the Darling Range towards Perth next morning, I roamed the corridor, hoping to find the old man, but came across Jim Brown instead. He looked different, clean-shaven and wearing a dark suit with a white business shirt and tie, but he also seemed to hold a sense of quiet purpose that I hadn't noticed before. I was turning away when he called after me, and I swung round to face him.

'I've got a message from your mate.' He was holding a small sheet of tightly folded paper.

'Where is he?'

'In the compartment.' He hesitated, as if puzzled. 'He must have told you all about it?'

'About what?'

'Jesus,' he said, and glanced at his watch. Pulling a small wallet from his pocket, he flipped it open to reveal a police badge.

I caught my breath. 'What's going on?'

He replaced the wallet and glanced along the empty corridor. 'It's been on TV and in all the papers. I'm taking him back to Perth for the inquest. You must have heard about it.'

'I've been overseas for years, and only just got back.'

He stared at me for a moment. 'There was some student trouble at the university. Your mate worked there…teaching something…poetry, maybe?'

'Student trouble?'

'You know – some kind of demonstration. These things get out of hand. Anyway, a girl got pushed down a flight of stairs. Broke her back. I'm not sure what part your mate played in it. As I said, I'm just taking him back.'

'You mean, he ran away?'

'Yeah. Bloody pathetic. Poor old sod like him. We found him in some doss house up the Cross. I had to bring him back by rail because he's got some medical problem with flying. He couldn't get off the train without me knowing about it, and he seemed to enjoy your company, so I thought I'd leave him alone as much as I could.' He paused and rubbed his ear. 'Jesus. The silly old bugger really didn't tell you anything?' He leant back against the window and grinned. 'What the bloody hell were you talking about all that time?'

I took the scrap of paper, knowing Jim Brown needn't have bothered to deliver it, or – for that matter – allowed the old man to spend so much time with me.

'Thanks,' I said.

He seemed embarrassed. 'No worries. And I didn't mean all that crap about poetry and poofters.' He paused. 'I was just…well, you know how it is on a long trip.'

'I know how it is.'

'Right,' he said briskly, turning away. 'I've got work to do. Cheers.'

I think I already knew what I'd find in the note, long before managing to smooth it flat and expose the single line of tightly academic handwriting. As the train eased into the city of Perth, with its vastly empty ocean beyond, I read the words aloud.

My soul, I whispered, beneath a steady beat of steel, is a strange country.

Down the Valley and Across the Sea

Mr Robinson woke suddenly and stared at the ceiling. It was not yet dawn but there was sufficient light for him to make out the cracked plastic lampshade with its dusty bulb. He listened carefully, trying to identify the sound that had roused him. As he waited, head cocked forward from the pillow and tilted slightly to one side, he watched his wife asleep beside him. Her mouth was open and she was breathing heavily, as if with conscious effort. She was dying.

Mrs Robinson had been dying for some time. Two years earlier, medical opinion had given her six months before the malignant and inoperable tumour claimed her life. Mr Robinson remembered the day precisely. He had been putting in long hours in the laboratory and had started to suffer eye strain and headaches. When his wife also complained, they had gone together to the hospital for examination. He had been given a new pair of glasses and she a death sentence. Six months. But two long years later she was still alive.

With medication and acceptance of a prospect of spiritual flight, Mrs Robinson had quickly surrendered to the morbid satisfaction of the doomed. She learned to exploit sympathy and never wasted an opportunity to gain further comfort for herself. Mr Robinson sometimes thought it would be a blessing if she were to hurry up and get on with her dying. But she lingered.

He listened for the noise that had woken him and heard it again, rumbling like distant surf. It seemed to come from a long way off, down the valley and across the sea; eluding definition and filling him with a curious sense of foreboding. He shivered and pulled the blankets up round his ears, hoping to muffle the sound, but still heard it. Global warming, he thought, and saw huge icebergs wallowing in rising seas, creaking and splintering before flooding the coastline...

'Did you hear anything this morning, dear?' he asked his wife at breakfast.

Mrs Robinson glanced up, annoyed to have her attention diverted from the plate of crispy bacon and poached eggs. She reached for the teapot. 'Hear anything?' she enquired with a sigh. 'What an insensitive question. You must know I hear everything. I haven't slept properly for years.'

Mr Robinson slid his knife across the single slice of toast on his plate. 'A kind of rumbling,' he said, avoiding her eyes. 'It woke me up.'

Mrs Robinson shuffled a large portion of egg, bacon and toast skilfully into her mouth and frowned. Taking a quick gulp of tea, she said, before the food had been entirely despatched, 'Rumbling? I heard no rumbling.' Then her lips curled in an ugly smile. 'Unless it came from your stomach.'

Next morning, Mr Robinson heard the noise again. Just before dawn, with his wife sleeping soundly by his side, he woke, hot and fearful, staring at the ceiling. The noise came from the same direction as before, down the valley and across the sea. Only this time it was closer. Once again he burrowed into the blankets to escape its searching urgency but it was futile. It's a bushfire, he thought, and saw the coastal plain ablaze with flame; trees exploding with heat while animals thumped and clawed the ground in panic.

'I heard it again this morning,' he told Mrs Robinson at breakfast.

She was pouring cream over a large dish of strawberries and paused. 'Heard what?'

'The noise,' he said, spreading a film of butter on his single slice of toast. 'I mentioned it yesterday.'

The spoon, heaped red and white, hesitated in front of Mrs Robinson's mouth. 'I think your ears are getting as bad as your eyes.'

Mr Robinson went back to his toast.

After breakfast, his wife asked him to pick up some more of the little red tablets from the chemist. 'You'll have to drop in and get a new prescription from Doctor Williamson first,' she said, rattling the newspaper.

Watching the doctor scribble on the prescription pad, Mr Robinson wondered if he should ask why his wife was still alive eighteen months after she was supposed to have died but, not knowing how to frame the question, remained silent.

Doctor Williamson closed his pad and looked up. 'I think Mrs Robinson has been avoiding me,' he said. 'It's time she came in for another examination.'

'Well,' replied Mr Robinson uncomfortably, 'it was difficult for her at first. You know…to accept that she was going to die. Having done so, I don't think she cares to consider the possibilities of a reprieve.'

The doctor handed over the prescription and stood up. 'We are all going to die, Mr Robinson. Some sooner, some later, but we are all going to die.'

Mr Robinson stood up, unable to think of a reply and the doctor steered him towards the door. 'Try to persuade her to come in and see me. There's a good chap.'

Mr Robinson nodded as he left.

In the chemist's shop, the pretty girl in the crisp white dress greeted him cheerfully. 'How's Mrs Robinson? I saw her in the supermarket the other day. Buying strawberries. She looked very well.'

Mr Robinson coughed to hide his surprise. He understood the grocery order was always phoned through and delivered because she was not strong enough to do the shopping herself.

Strolling home, he began to feel uneasy. The day was warm and soft, with a tight blue sky, on which someone had daubed a few hasty clouds. The billowing whiteness reminded him of something and eventually he remembered the lush heap of cream disappearing into his wife's mouth.

Passing a thick hedge, a thorn snagged the chemist's paper bag, tearing it open and spilling the bottle of tablets. He reached down to pick it up and noticed the word 'Caution' marked boldly in red. He placed the bottle in his pocket and looked up at the fat white clouds again.

The following morning, he heard the noise once more. It had crossed the sea and was now in the valley. A curious, chant-like cadence quite unlike anything he could imagine.

After breakfast, he prepared Mrs Robinson's medicine. Taking twenty of the little red tablets, he carefully crushed them into a fine powder and put them in the teapot. His wife liked a pot of tea with her medication. About noon, he called the doctor and said he thought Mrs Robinson was ill. The ambulance arrived and took her away. The house became very quiet.

That evening, Mr Robinson was listening to his jazz records for the first time in years when the telephone rang. It was Doctor Williamson.

'I'm afraid it seems your wife has taken an overdose – '

' – one moment please, Doctor,' interrupted Mr Robinson, putting down the receiver and adjusting the volume on the stereo.

' – it's understandable, I suppose,' the doctor was saying when Mr Robinson picked up the receiver again, 'but strange that she should have waited so long. Have you noticed any depression lately?'

'I don't think so.'

'Have you spoken to the hospital this evening?'

Mr Robinson shifted in his chair. 'No.'

'Oh, this will come as a surprise, then. I took the opportunity to run a few tests and the results are extraordinary.' The doctor paused and Mr Robinson waited silently. 'Your wife's tumour, Mr Robinson, seems to have vanished completely.'

In the silence that followed, the doctor said, 'Mr Robinson? Are you still there? I know this is a shock. A happy one nevertheless. Your wife is strong and healthy. There's no reason why she shouldn't return home tomorrow.'

'Thank you,' said Mr Robinson and replaced the receiver.

In the morning, he stared at the ceiling. The noise was crashing up the valley towards him. Like a screaming, stumbling madman it came, bursting into the house and rushing up the corridor for the bedroom. He raised a hand in futile protest as it smashed through the door, thundered across his forehead, and reached unerringly for the two-year-old malignant tumour in his brain.

A Balance of Probabilities

> Burst like a star: for here there is
> no place that does not see you.
> You must change your life.
>
> – Rainer Maria Rilke

The flame wavered, steadied, then bunched in a sleek, yellow plume, like the hood of some exotic snake. She stared into it until her eyelids became heavy, then reached for the knife. The steel was cold and masked the sting of the first cut. Warm blood seeped darkly over white flesh as she changed hands, sliding the blade across her left wrist. This time it hurt but now the worst part was over. She let the knife drop from her fingers and sat, lotus-like, staring into the candle flame at eye level on the coffee table before her. A feeling of stillness she hadn't known for years held her calm. The room, outside the pale light, was dim, its familiar shapes becoming irrelevant as consciousness ebbed away. She was nineteen years old, and the note on the table simply said, 'This life has been discontinued due to lack of interest.'

*

Canvas cracked in the wind like a gunshot as he called, 'Do you hate my guts?'

Lucinda narrowed her eyes against the shining water. 'I don't think so.'

'Not even a minor intestine?'

'Maybe your appendix.'

'I had it out. Years ago.'

She smiled. 'I know.'

He pushed the tiller away. 'Coming about!'

She ducked as the boom swung across, mainsail flapping and halyards wriggling through pulleys like frantic silkworms. The dinghy settled back on course.

'Seriously, though, I'd understand if you did.'

Busy securing the jib sheet, she glanced back. 'Did what?'

'Hate my guts.'

Jesus, she thought, men's guilt is almost as boring as their chauvinism. She arched her body out over the water as they picked up speed again and began to heel. Above her the sails curved away, taut, like the wings of a giant butterfly pinned to an empty sky.

'Sorry, Steve.' she called. 'It's difficult to hate anyone on a day like this.'

He was staring at the mainsail, his mouth tugged down at the corners.

Shit! she thought, I've said the wrong thing again. Moving her foot, she nudged him playfully on the shin. 'It's okay. Really it is. I do understand.'

Their eyes met, and he smiled. She saw the strong, white teeth, wide shoulders above tanned muscular flesh and thought, Right here in the sunlight and sea spray it would be easy to say, 'Bugger the rest of the world, let's think only of ourselves.' But she didn't.

That night, in bed together, she tried to recapture the mood.

'You know,' he was saying, giving a long and satisfied sigh, 'we're good for each other.'

She looked down at him through half-closed eyes, her hands on his shoulders, thinking, That's certainly true in your case, with an empty, wifeless bed at home. She said, 'Has she gone for good this time?'

He stared at her breasts in front of his face as if they held some important secret. 'This time,' he said, 'it won't make any difference.'

She began to move, matching his increasing urgency. 'Jesus,' he breathed, as if making a religious conversion, 'Cinda, you're fucking marvellous.'

Coming out of the library, she bumped into Rhonda and remembered the meeting. 'Oh shit! I'm sorry, Ron. The Action Committee. I got caught up. How did it go?'

Rhonda laughed without amusement. 'That silly bitch Sasha was elected. Sasha! Sounds like a bloody curtain cord, doesn't it? What does she know? She thinks the feminist movement begins and ends with *The Female Eunuch*.'

'Can I buy you a coffee as penance?'

Rhonda shook her head. 'Your vote wouldn't have made any difference. I'm late for a lecture. See you at lunch?' She hesitated, and Rhonda asked, 'Are you still seeing Steve?'

'It's okay. I know what I'm doing.'

'I hope so, Cinda. Look what happened last time.' Rhonda's voice softened. 'I saw your poem in the rag. It was great! Is it from the collection?'

'Yes.'

'Any word from the publisher yet?'

'Not yet.' She pulled a face. 'No one reads poetry now.'

'No one reads, full stop.' Rhonda attempted an encouraging smile. 'But stick with it, kid. They tell me talent always wins through in the end.' She glanced at her watch. 'God! I'm late. Must fly. See you at lunch?' Rhonda was moving away, looking back, expecting an answer, but she made no reply.

She bears the pain of ages,
She does not question why.
She just turns and turns the pages,
And wonders how to die.

'…Rhonda. Wait!'

But it was too late. The compact figure, with its freckled face and bobbing red hair, had vanished.

She toyed with her wine glass as Steve recounted a recent promotion. 'You should have seen the pompous sods, Cinda. The ponce who called me into the interview room inspected my shoes and then did a slow pan upwards, as if I was a tailor's dummy. I began to worry about the state of my underpants.'

She smiled on cue but he frowned and said, 'I hope I'm not boring you?'

She met his eyes and lied easily. 'Of course not.' Letting her hand fall below the table, she squeezed his knee. 'But you've got to get back to the office and I've another tutorial. We're wasting valuable time.'

That night, sprawled on cushions and sharing a joint, Rhonda said, 'I really can't think what you see in him.'

Lucinda was trying to open a bottle of wine and giggled. 'He can do this better than I can.'

'Here,' demanded Rhonda, 'give it to me. You're destroying the cork.'

'The story of my life.'

Rhonda opened the bottle and found two glasses. 'Are these clean?'

'They were last time we used them.'

They sipped and smoked for a while, then Rhonda said, 'Do you know there's talk of petitioning the Chancellor about sexual blackmail?'

Lucinda coughed on the wine. 'What?'

'Apparently a tutor has been giving good marks for sex.'

'How does he grade it?'

Rhonda frowned. 'It's not funny.'

Lucinda leant back, watching the marijuana smoke trickle upwards. 'Isn't it? Sex always struck me as having great comic potential.'

'Not in this context.'

'It's just another form of communication.'

'What is?'

'Sex. It's merely a currency – '

'Currency!' Rhonda's voice became angry. 'Are you condoning tutors who trade marks for sexual favours?'

'It depends.'

'On what?'

'On the currency.' She began to giggle again. 'What he's got to offer.'

Rhonda stared in horror for a moment, but then began to giggle herself, and soon they were both rolling on the floor helpless with laughter. A wine glass broke and cut into flesh and they crawled into the bathroom, Rhonda knocking bottles off shelves and shrieking, 'There's no first aid. You'll have to settle for second.'

Lucinda stood at the bathroom sink, watching the surrealist patterns of blood on white enamel, and bit her lip. 'The story of my life again.'

Later, with her hand wrapped in a towel, they finished the wine and the marijuana.

That winter she went home to her parents for a few days. The paddocks were green with clover, and water in the top dam lapped the entrance to the small cave where she hid to write poetry on hot and lonely schoolgirl days. Her mother's expression of resigned martyrdom was unchanged. Her father, big, slow and inarticulate, regarded her sadly whenever she met his eyes. The dinner-table dialogue was flinty and barren; she might have been a distant relative rather than the only child on a rare visit.

Once upon a time warp,
I heard a robin sing.
He sang of winters long ago,
And marmalade with string.

Her mother said, 'I found some photos the other day. Of you in your first school uniform. A sports day, I think. Perhaps it was a fete – '

' – worse than death?' The interruption was instinctive and instantly regretted.

Her mother began collecting plates as if nothing had been said and her father took out his pipe.

'What will you do?' he asked quietly, 'when you've finished with your books?'

'When I have my degree? I'm not sure. I haven't really thought about it.'

Her mother made a disapproving click with her tongue as she disappeared into the kitchen, and her father began the slow ritual of lighting his pipe.

She watched, remembering how, as a child, she would be allowed to blow out the match. 'How are you, dad?'

The giant hand paused, cradling the tiny flame like a tabernacle before crushing it in a closed fist. 'Not so bad,' he replied between puffs. 'Could use some help around the farm, of course.' He paused and met her eyes. 'As could your mother, no doubt.'

She looked away. 'Don't. You know I had to leave.'

'Had to?'

'I couldn't go to university around here, could I?'

'Will you come back?'

'After my degree. Perhaps.'

He shook his head. 'Too late.'

She felt a sting of tears. 'Too late for what?'

'For the farm.' He stood up. 'I'll be on the veranda for a while.'

She knew. As a child, she would go and sit with him, but tonight she remained at the table. Alone. Head bowed and choking back a sadness thick enough to suffocate her.

Next morning, before breakfast, she walked up to the top dam. The farmhouse roof, glimpsed below her through the trees, seemed closer than she recalled, but the road beyond still wandered away like a piece of dusty string. Long ago, she would watch and wait, hoping desperately for a car to appear and turn in at the gate. It never did. Today, the road remained empty. The world, apparently, had not come any closer. When she said goodbye, a few days later, she knew she would never return.

The following weekend, she drove to the coast with Steve. They stayed at a friend's beach house. There was sand on the floor and dust on the furniture, the refrigerator stank and possums crashed about in the roof.

During the night there was a violent storm and the rumbling surf kept her awake. Just before dawn, it became very calm and, leaving Steve still sleeping, she went for a long walk on the beach. The sea looked benign. Had she dreamt last night's waves?

She found several dead birds and three heavy posts buried upright in the sand. It was some time before she realised they must have been washed in, spearing off huge breakers with the force of a sledgehammer, impaling shellfish and seaweed like lances. Now they stood erect; spent, misplaced and slightly ridiculous, like the ruins of some ancient, tribal fortress. She rested against one of them and stared at the sea. It was mottled green and blue in the storm's aftermath, and near the horizon charcoal grey, as if from a savage bruise. She pushed her shoulder against the post but it failed to move.

The sun was rising and the colour of the sky brightened. A keening sense of disconnection bore down on her with such isolating force her feet began to sink into the sand with the posts. She cried out, as if in pain, and ran all the way back to the beach house. Steve was still asleep. She made some coffee and wondered how to leave.

'You can be a selfish little bitch sometimes, Cinda.'

'What? I thought you wanted me to stop seeing him.'

Rhonda sipped her coffee primly. 'That was before I knew he was getting a divorce.'

'Shit! That wasn't because of me. His marriage was stuffed ages ago. Before he even met me.' She paused, and looked at her friend in amazement. 'Anyhow, what difference would a divorce make?'

'It might mean a lot. You might get married – '

'I don't believe this! You told me marriage was a myth. Little more than domestic slavery.'

Rhonda put down her coffee cup and glanced around the near-empty refectory. 'There's no need to shout, Cinda. I'm only being realistic.'

'Realistic! You wouldn't know reality if it leapt up and bit you on the bum! Jesus! You make me want to puke! What about the movement?'

'It's not about men versus women, Cinda. There's nothing wrong with marriage per se. The problem is the introduction of genuine equality, and the need to deconstruct social stereotypes.'

'Don't quote basic sociology at me, Rhonda. I've got a headache.'

'But what if he genuinely loves you? What then?'

'You bloody hypocrite. You said love was a Hollywood fantasy. Love! You know even less about love than you do about reality.'

There was a short, tense silence, then Rhonda stood up. Her voice was low and she was close to tears. 'You have no right to say that, Cinda. I thought we understood each other well enough for you to know what I was talking about. We all need love, no matter how we define it. We all need it, though. To that extent – although you may think otherwise – you're no different from the rest of the rabble.' She turned and, with solemn dignity, walked away.

Lucinda remained at the table. It was as if she had been kicked in the stomach by a runaway horse. She wanted to call Rhonda back but couldn't move. She stared at her coffee, knowing there was only one solution. That night, alone in her room, she wrote the single-line note, lit the candle and reached for the knife. As someone once said, When you think about life, you dream of revenge…

… Water in the top dam lapped at the entrance to the small cave. Below, among the trees, the tin roof shone in the sun like a beacon. Beyond the trees the empty road rolled away to a green-brown distance, like a discarded memory. But the road wasn't empty. A car was approaching, slowing and turning in at the gate. Opening her eyes, she saw her mother.

*

Postal service to the island was a hit or miss affair. The letter came by truck from the city to the coast, then by ferry to the island, and, at the whim of Kyroukis, a local fisherman, eventually found its way to the whitewashed stone cottage on the hill above the rocky bay.

She sat by a small table in the shade, looking out over the sea towards Crete. The letter was from Rhonda and she read it aloud.

Dearest Lucinda,

I finished your novel in one breathless (almost) gulp, and recognised a lot of people including myself (but don't worry, I'm not going to sue). I saw your mother last week and she told me your father is much better. They are both very proud of you, of course. Your mother got a bit emotional remembering that night at uni when I just managed to get you to hospital. It's embarrassing how she keeps thanking me – I told you about the extravagant house warming present she gave Sasha and me, didn't I? Your mum – poor thing – kept looking for a man around the house. But I digress. She never saw the note. No one did, except me. I don't suppose you even remember what you wrote but I shall keep it locked away, so that when you and I are gone, the National Library will be able to show it to your biographer. I can tell from your novel that you have worked it out. It seems a long time ago in many ways but sometimes, when I'm at the uni, it could be yesterday…

She let the pages slip from her grasp and looked up. Late-afternoon sun had beaten the Aegean Sea into a gleaming sheet of pewter. Turning to where the shadows deepened, she asked, 'Do you think I've worked it out?'

'Worked what out?'

She thought for a moment then shrugged. 'I'm not sure there's a name for it. Something to do with distance.'

'I hope not,' came the reply, 'because when you do you're going to be a lot less interesting.'

'But happier, perhaps?'

'Aren't you happy enough now?'

She stared at the sea before reaching down for Rhonda's letter. Then, clearing her throat, she began to read again.

…do you remember the dam and the little cave where you used to write poetry? Your mother told me it was flooded last winter and collapsed. When she went up to have a look, the hillside seemed to have reshaped itself. As if the cave had never existed…

Not Remembering Michael

A parable for our time

> I and the public know
> What all school children learn,
> Those to whom evil is done
> Do evil in return.
>
> – W.H. Auden (1907–1973)

What are we going to do about your father's ashes? Jane asks, having searched the hall cupboard for a missing bath towel and found the funeral urn.

I turn away. Michael didn't believe in ritual. When I was a child, long before we fled to Australia, he told me to believe whatever I liked, providing it wasn't a lie. Because a lie unravels the world, he whispered, having quickly unravelled my clumsy attempt to reconstruct a half-truth; which is ironic, because I now suspect the world is held together by lies, and in order to live as if part of something greater than ourselves we must somehow reconcile the cruelty and chaos of religious myth.

And yet…and yet, there must be something that connects our pitiful self-interest with a higher plane. Perhaps it's the God behind the God we don't believe; the God we haven't yet discovered. My father was an Irish Catholic, but I was never sure if he believed in any God. He claimed we should live out our own narrative, based on freedom, justice and humanity, and would open a dog-eared book of poetry, a relic from his secret days on the lonely west coast of Ireland, and shout a line from Yeats: Everything exists, everything is true, and the earth is only a little dust under our feet.

I now suspect existence and truth are mostly illusions shaped by context, since we have always been prisoners of perception. We don't see things as they are, we see them as we are, and Michael's perception as an Irish terrorist was forged at the age of nine in the burning crucible of having to watch his father die at the family kitchen table in Belfast;

a huge, strong man, choking on his own blood after being shot at close range by a Royalist religious fanatic. Seven years later, Michael joined the IRA. You don't forgive or forget something like that, he told me, and I received the scar without qualification, like a baton passing from one generation to the next. However, in what he liked to call – perhaps whimsically – a small act of kindness, Michael steadfastly refused to take part in any IRA operation outside of Ireland, often to his own cost.

Now, a lifetime later, in gathering spirals of inherited hatred, played out against the backdrop of wider conflicts, reflected nightly on family television screens in self-righteous accusations of evil, tossed back and forth – like a frantic game of pass the parcel – in endless loops between right-wing Christian arrogance and fundamentalist Islamic extremism, there is widespread despair at the prospect of resolution.

What will it take, I ask, prompted by Michael's ashes, to break the circuit?

I thought she was asleep, but Jane's clear response floats up from the darkness: Empathy.

I wait for something more, but it doesn't come. How would that work?

By imagining your enemy's pain to allow forgiveness.

Impossible, I reply, remembering Michael's father.

Not impossible, Jane says, if drip-fed in small acts of kindness.

I give a surprised gasp of recognition at the words. Why small?

She kisses me lightly on the side of my face, and I sense the fact that she is smiling. Because they're more likely to slip in under the radar.

We lay tangled in the same bed in which our children were conceived; two boys and a girl, now with families of their own, somewhere out there, each in search of staying whole in a fragmenting world.

But is it really that simple? I ask; whispering, as if afraid to crack the fragility of a shared secret.

Yes, she whispers in reply, if we can allow ourselves to let it be.

Early next morning, we scatter Michael's ashes on an outgoing tide, with rain clouds pressing away from Melbourne towards the Bass Strait.

Maybe he'll reach Tasmania, Jane says, as we return the empty urn to the boot of our car.

I think he'd prefer Ireland, I reply, glancing back at the sea. He always reckoned it hadn't done with him.

Safely home in the companionable silence of our kitchen, over tea and marmalade toast, Jane says quietly, as if we were still on the beach, Yes, Ben, Ireland has done with him. Don't you see? That's another thing about a small act of kindness. Not having to remember from where it came.

Existentialism and the Friday Night Syndrome

You know the feeling. It begins every Friday lunchtime and gradually expands with delicious seduction all afternoon. By four o'clock, the brain is slipping out of its weekday wardrobe and into something comfortable. The weekend looms ahead, beckoning with promise. But somewhere between that promise and the last gasp of the working week exists a kind of no-man's land; an absolute transition point where everything pauses before bearing away on a new tack. Here, momentarily, your defences are down and, like a boxer who has lowered his guard, you are vulnerable. And anything is possible.

Bruce calls it the Friday Night Syndrome. 'That's what it's all about really,' he says, slopping his beer across the bar.

I move my sleeve just in time. 'What is?' I ask, regarding him cautiously from the sanctity of my schooner.

'What old John Paul was on about, you dopey drongo.' He pauses to guzzle half a schooner, watching me all the time with his dog-brown eyes. Then he drags the back of a hand across his mouth, belches softly and says, 'Nothing can be proved, only shown.'

A Saturday afternoon smoke haze shrouds the public bar as punters study the racing form, followed by the barmaid's form, and complete the trifecta by checking the odds on a TV set growing from the wall.

A shapeless mass insinuates the space between Bruce and myself. With a squawk like a mating mongoose, it yelps, 'Whose shout?'

'Yours, you big fat bastard,' comes the friendly chorus from across the room.

My view of Bruce is totally eclipsed, so I take a cold mouthful of beer and consider the proposition. Last week, Bruce had watched an SBS profile of Jean-Paul Sartre under the mistaken impression it was a French skin flick. Eventually realising his error, he discovered the TV remote control batteries were flat and, being the lazy sod he is, couldn't be bothered standing up to change channels. Seeing this as a lay-down misère for existentialism, Bruce had pulled the out of fashion philosophy on like a pair of old footy shorts.

The Big Fat Bastard is ordering a fleet of schooners and I realise Bruce is still sending signals from the dark side of the mass. 'Existentialism,' I hear, neatly bracketed by a broken belch, 'is more than just an attempt to grasp reality.'

The Big Fat Bastard swivels on his axis. 'If you ask me, mate, you've been grasping it too much already.'

Bruce ignores this editorial comment and peers at me through a hairy armpit. 'Will infinity last?' he wants to know.

'Only time will tell,' I respond on cue.

But Bruce shakes his head. Or I think he shakes his head. It's hard to tell through a hairy armpit. Anyway, he rabbits on, 'John Paul's first principle. Remember? Existence precedes Essence.'

I can't think of a reply. The Big Fat Bastard spins into orbit clutching a honeycomb of beer and muttering something about the place being full of friggin' poofters. Bruce doesn't notice, assumes he's still got a hairy armpit to contend with, and shouts unnecessarily into empty space, 'There's no such thing as absolute truth.'

I sip my beer. 'But if that's true, then there is.'

Bruce goes glassy-eyed and I play my trump card: 'And if there is, then the statement isn't true.' I lean back, feeling pleased with myself. 'A pretty paradox, n'est ce pas?'

Bruce is unimpressed. 'Stuff ya flamin' paradox. I'm talking about the Friday Night Syndrome. I can prove it.'

'Prove what?' I ask, losing interest. 'That nothing can be proved?'

Bruce blinks a couple of times, as if surprised to see me again, then waves a hand impatiently. 'I can prove, you bloody drongo, the link between existentialism and the Friday Night Syndrome.' He swallows the rest of his beer. 'Explanations, explanations, that's all you bloody intellectual cripples ever want. Where's your imagination? Your curiosity? Your…' His voice tapers into silence as the barmaid's creamy breasts swing across his line of sight. The experience seems to suggest a new thought. 'Sylvia,' he says, cautiously at first, and then with greater certainty, 'Sylvia. Yes, that's it. Sylvia.'

'What about Sylvia?' I ask suspiciously (Sylvia being a recently commenced research project of my own that I don't fancy sharing with Bruce).

'That's how we prove the link exists,' he replies, as if the connection was obvious. Then he notices my anxiety and adds, 'Don't worry, mate. It's purely in the interests of metaphysical research.'

I watch the barmaid saunter away. 'You wouldn't notice a bucket of metaphysical research if someone tipped it on your head.'

Bruce looks hurt and doesn't speak for two-point-five schooners (in real time about seven minutes). It's an impressive, but vaguely disturbing, achievement.

Then he sticks out his chin and says, 'I've got fifty bucks that says you're not game.'

I think about it. It seems futile to remind him that I have no theory to prove. In fact, I'm not at all sure what the stuff he's talking about. But Bruce, after a few Saturday afternoon schooners, is not easily fobbed off.

'Okay,' I reply, with a what-the-hell shrug, 'I'm listening.'

Bruce orders another round and I slip into the boozy, mellow world of metaphysical mateship, where the optional extras, such as knowing when to leave, have been removed.

On Monday, I phone Sylvia, and we agree to meet for dinner on Friday night.

'How about a drink at my place first?' I ask. She pauses and I wonder if she's thinking what I think she's thinking. She says, 'That's a nice idea. What time?'

Attempting sophistication, I say casually, 'How about seven-thirty for eight?' But she asks, 'Eight what?' and I say, 'Don't worry. I'll see you at seven-thirty. Okay?'

'Okay.' Sylvia is in Marilyn-speak mode (which tends to make her sound a bit like a thirsty sheepdog with laryngitis). 'I'll look forward to it.'

During the week I have second thoughts. Sylvia is fiery-tempered and if she suspects conspiracy the reprisals don't bear thinking about. Friday arrives on schedule and I prepare the scene carefully but with apprehension. I sense it's going to be a disaster, but can't see why. It worries me like an itch impossible to scratch.

Bruce had advised, Put some music on. You know, something existential. How about the final movement of Schubert's *Unfinished Symphony*? I'd suggested with a grin, but he'd replied, straight-faced, Yeah, that should do the trick.

In the event I don't play music. For one thing it would make Sylvia skittish. She's a one-dimensional girl and enjoys her food with singular enthusiasm, preferring to eat without delay or decoration. I twitch as the doorbell sounds.

She is wearing something blue that shimmers down over her breasts like a fabled waterfall as she wafts into the room on the best part of a bottle of French perfume I'd given her the week before. Her long, auburn hair shines in the low light and her white teeth gleam as she says, 'When do we eat, darling. I'm starved.'

'Sylvia, why don't you do the Third World a favour and fast for a couple of hours?'

Her lips part in a glossy smile that suggests she is wondering if the Third World is the second planet on the left past Jupiter, or the restaurant I have chosen for the evening. 'Are you suggesting I eat too much?

'Not for a racing camel – ' I begin, but sense danger as her eyebrows arch. 'Of course, there's nothing wrong with a healthy appetite.'

She pouts. 'I'm a growing girl.'

I glance at my watch to obliterate the vision of a larger Sylvia. It's time to launch the Bruce plan. 'Sylvia, have you heard of existentialism?'

She frowns. 'Is it some kind of religion?'

It's closer than I thought she'd get first go. I smile. 'Try philosophy.'

'Philosophy?'

I nod. 'The search for a link between being and existence...or between you and me.'

'What kind of philosophy is that?'

'Existentialism.'

'Isn't that some kind of religion?'

Barely managing to suppress impatience, I say, 'This is where we came in. Why don't you sit down and loosen your dress?'

'Loosen my dress?'

I begin to sweat. Christ! Did I really say that? 'Well, you're not wearing a tie.'

She remains standing. Time and fate hang in the balance.

Then she says slowly, as if confronted by an idiot child, 'Would you mind telling me exactly what we are talking about?'

I take a breath. 'Existentialism. That's philosophy, not religion. And I just thought, in the interests of metaphysical research, we might try reversing the order of circumstance.'

Her eyes widen. 'Perhaps I should go out and come back in. This isn't making any sense at all.'

'Existence precedes essence,' I say encouragingly, 'you know. Perhaps we should get it out of the way first.'

'Get what out of the way?'

'It.'

She stares at me blankly. 'It?'

'You know...the, er, sex thing.'

This is the moment, I tell myself. Intrinsic truth as opposed to absolute truth. The Bruce plan says sex is okay after dinner, after the soft lights, the food and the booze, and maybe a few half-hearted refusals to show that they're not that sort of girl. Except for Friday nights...when, according to Bruce, existentialism comes into play.

I turn away, fumbling for words, and hear a brief rustle of silk. Swinging back, I see that Sylvia is wearing nothing but a pair of slingback stilettos, stockings and a black lace suspender belt.

‘A quickie before dinner is fine by me,’ she says, advancing with mesmerising fluency.

It’s funny, but somehow a naked Sylvia manages to look more naked than any naked woman I have ever seen. She is more than the sum of her moving parts. I’m a closet feminist but if Sylvia *en déshabillé* isn’t the mother of all sex objects, then Jean-Paul Sartre never had breakfast with Simone de Beauvoir. Logic shrivels in the face of such a truth.

Suddenly, her fingers are opening my shirt and I’m whispering, ‘But Sylvia, we don’t have to rush things. You won’t respect me afterwards.’

She is breathing into my ear. ‘Nonsense, we mustn’t be late for dinner.’ And then she adds, her lips brushing my neck, ‘Close your eyes and think of existentialism.’

Suspended in the mystical shroud of a Saturday afternoon public bar, Bruce watches me with the eyes of a drugged owl. His beer hand, normally the steadiest limb he possesses, is trembling as he moans, ‘For Chrissakes, don’t stop. Then what happens?’

I swallow a cold mouthful of beer. ‘Nothing.’

‘Nothing?’

‘Nothing.’

‘Oh come on, mate,’ he wails, ‘you’re telling me Sylvia’s standing there with just her boarding lights on and nothing happens?’

I look away.

Bruce is silent for a long time. Then gives a heavy, theatrical sigh and flags down a passing schooner.

The bet remains unresolved. Bruce drops Jean-Paul and shacks up with Sylvia. Perhaps this was the real plan all along, but how could I have missed it? Maybe there’s a case for an existentialist revival after all. However, I suspect it will all become academic. If Sylvia goes on eating at her present rate, she’ll move in with the Big Fat Bastard. Which suggests chaos theory rather than existentialism. But I doubt if Bruce would see it that way.

King's Gambit

'Do you remember old Watkins?'

I nod vaguely. 'Sidelined years ago, wasn't he? I suppose he's dead now.'

'Died only last week, as a matter of fact. Found with a bottle of pills. Obviously topped himself, but no sign of a note.' He pauses to make sure I am listening. 'They looked everywhere but found nothing. A mystery. There'd been no evidence of depression and he was in good health apart from the normal restrictions of old age. Then someone noticed the chessboard. It was set up as if for a game but none of the pieces had been moved. Except for the white king. It was tipped on its side.' He smiles. 'The old bastard hadn't suicided, he'd just resigned.'

I rouse myself from post-dinner stupor.

My companion is setting up the board. 'Another game?'

I hesitate. 'I'm not really in your class.'

'Nonsense. Chess isn't about winning or losing.'

I smile, thinking, Not if you win as often as you do. 'I wasn't aware that Watkins played chess.'

'Oh yes. He was a damned fine player. Mind you, he always found the going tough against the new breed.' He sniffs disapprovingly and gives a sidelong glance at the dozen or so chess club members hunched over their boards. 'The hypermoderns. Gain a pawn then let technique win, instead of imagination.'

He shakes his head and places a pair of knights. 'Old Watkins was made of different stuff. He liked to play the King's Gambit. When did you last see that used in here? No. And you're not likely to either. Too romantic, the hypermoderns say. Too risky, they mean.' His face softens. 'I particularly remember a double rook sacrifice Watkins played in a tournament years ago. Forced mate in twelve. I'll never forget the expression on the other chap's face.'

He leans back and sighs. 'That sort of play is missed. Watkins is missed.'

'A mind like that must have been useful in the Section.'

He sits forward again and slaps down a bishop. 'I would have recruited only chess players.'

I smile. 'You ran the Section virtually by yourself in those days, didn't you?'

He nods, pleased at the memory. 'And I had some damned fine players.' He gives a sudden chuckle. 'We'd communicate in chess moves. Like something out of *Alice Through the Looking Glass*.' His face clouds. 'But one by one they left us and went on to bigger and better things, leaving only Watkins and me from the old team. The new chaps were clever, of course, some of them with brilliant degrees, but they tended to think the Sicilian Defence was something Rommel tried in West Africa. I never found another Watkins.'

'Wasn't he involved in the Beirut incident?'

'Yes. Funny you should mention it. I was going through the papers only this afternoon. For the book, you know. I came across his report. Beautiful stuff – pure Watkins – but I don't suppose I could use it.'

'Why on earth not?'

He shrugs. 'Might cause a bit of a flap.'

I laugh. 'There's nothing like a bit of a flap to help sell a book.'

He frowns, and I realise I've made an error of judgement. 'If the book sells,' he says carefully, 'it will certainly not be because of controversy.'

I stare at the board, mentally biting my tongue. The pieces are all in place, with white on my side, but I make no move. I am pleasantly comfortable after a good dinner and a glass of brandy and feel disinclined to concentrate against one of the club's best players. I'd much rather hear the Beirut story, but suspect I've missed my chance.

But it's worth another try. 'When you say "pure Watkins", you leave me a little in the dark. You must remember, I hardly knew him.'

He is studying the board, anticipating my opening move. Then he looks up quickly and I know the ploy has worked. 'Well, as you know,' he begins, leaning back again, 'Watkins was sent to Beirut to investigate the rumour we had an Israeli spy on the locally engaged embassy staff.'

I nod. 'Head of Mission driver, as I recall.'

'Yes. That made the job a bit tricky. The driver had been employed for almost fifteen years and become something of a favourite. The ambassador at the post when Watkins arrived was particularly fond of our man. Used to drive the wife to the shops, kids to school and fetch and carry a few personal items now and then. That sort of thing.'

I knew the sort of thing. It keeps the Department on the back foot before Public Accounts Committees.

My companion continues. 'Watkins soon discovered the rumour had substance. The driver had been giving stuff to Mossad for years. He was a Druze Arab and had family in Israel. This was the late sixties, of course, and Beirut was still a beautiful city, not the pile of rubble it soon became, and Lebanon wasn't really interested in taking on Jerusalem. They only sent two Hawker Hunters up in the six-day war. One of 'em got shot down and the other hightailed it back to base. That was their contribution to Arab airborne solidarity. But Beirut had always been a nest of spies and the driver, because of his diplomatic connection, was nicely placed to gather the odd snippet or two for Israeli intelligence.'

He gives the room a sideways glance. It's quiet and we are tucked away in a corner. There is little chance of being overheard, even in the unlikely event that anyone is interested, but he lowers his voice. 'So, Watkins had a problem. Obviously he couldn't just blow the whistle. There'd have been a diplomatic ruckus that could have jeopardised our standing in the Middle East. The driver would have to go, but for what reason? He was an excellent employee and well liked by senior diplomats.' His face releases a thin smile. 'And you know how your cocktail party types tend to look down their noses at my people.' He shrugs at the memory. 'I've seen some of your Third Secretaries spend all day clipping stories from local newspapers.'

I make no comment. Distance between diplomat and spy is elastic, often resting on tenuous circumstance.

He settles back and continues. 'Obviously, no one from the embassy knew the real reason for Watkins being there. The cover story was a routine security check.' He meets my eyes. 'Of course, Watkins could have simply framed the driver on a stealing charge, or something similar, and given the embassy a clear reason to dismiss him. That's what the book would have recommended.'

He is silent for a while, and his expression becomes reflective. 'You know,' he says eventually, 'Watkins told me he only prepared for a chess tournament once. He'd been drawn against a well-known exponent of the Sicilian Defence, and spent days swotting up on book theory. He became so focused on the Sicilian that when the fellow played an obscure variation of the Grunfeld, poor old Watkins went blank. There was a routine combination in the centre involving an exchange of queens but, when the dust settled, Watkins found himself two pawns down. He was shattered and lost badly. He threw away book theory after that and relied on instinct and imagination. It's risky. Tournaments are more to do with reputation than prizes, and miscalculation can bring disgrace as well as defeat. But the satisfaction of winning a game you have crafted for yourself, rather than sweated out of some damned book is something special.'

There is another long pause, during which he stares down at the board. But I know he isn't thinking about our uncommenced game. When he speaks, I have guessed what he is going to say.

'So that's how Watkins took on Beirut. Not by book theory but imagination. He played the King's Gambit.'

I wait. The room seems to have shrunk to the point where we are the only occupants.

'And what do you suppose he used as the king's bishop pawn?'

'I've no idea.'

He smiles. 'A damned great box of expensive cigars.'

He sips his brandy with approval and stretches his legs. 'Havanas. The ambassador couldn't resist them, apparently. The embassy constantly reeked of stale smoke. Everyone complained. But not to the old man's face. They wouldn't dare. Inside the embassy, he was a tyrant. Ran the place like a ship at sea. A warship. And he was in command. The first secretary, a good diplomat but spineless, was his executive officer, and the vice consul the bosun. The vice consul, you may remember, was a bit of a larrikin and knew the black market backwards. He'd get the ambassador's supply of fresh Havanas from a seedy part of town the old boy didn't wish to know about. He just paid his monthly account, reimbursed himself from the official slush fund and puffed happily away. The vice consul did quite nicely out of it, too, but that's another story.'

It was indeed another story, and I remembered the vice consul well. He'd returned home under threat of currency regulation charges and, despite importing a Mercedes purchased from proceeds of probable corruption, had been kicked upstairs with a couple of quick promotions before early retirement. Last I heard, he was comfortably placed with the respectable charisma of a diplomatic career behind him and a future in expensive real estate in front.

My companion resumes his story. 'Our man, the head of mission driver, I'll call him Jacob –that's not his name but will do for our purposes – well, Jacob was sometimes allowed to drive the official car home in the evening and park in the street outside his flat. There was a spare set of keys kept in the embassy and, on the evening of such an arrangement, Watkins nabbed them.'

Someone wanders near our table, notices the game has not commenced and pauses as if about to speak. My companion glances up and shakes his head, and the passer-by moves on without a word. Even here, the man sitting opposite me is respected for his calm sense of authority. I am one of the few people in the club who understands something of the ruthless, single-minded qualities that have made him such a professional success.

Waiting until we are alone again, he continues. 'The car keys weren't the only things Watkins took that day. Earlier, he had pinched a box of the ambassador's cigars. He identified the Mossad agent controller through the local network, and sent him the cigars with a note of thanks for letting Australian Intelligence share Jacob. Late that night, Watkins took the ambassador's car from Jacob's street, drove it across town and parked outside the flat of a woman journalist who had been freelancing for the CIA. After giving Mossad time to note the car's presence, Watkins returned it to the exact spot he had taken it from. As far as he could tell, Jacob was totally unaware the car had been moved.'

He lifts his brandy glass again and, although reluctant to disturb the flow of his narrative, I feel compelled to speak. 'Surely you're not suggesting Mossad would believe such a proposition? That Jacob was also working for Australian Intelligence? They would have questioned him.'

My companion smiles indulgently. 'And Jacob would, of course, deny it since it was untrue. But Mossad would expect him to deny it and soon begin to wonder if he had been compromised. It's all shadows in this game, you know. Shadows and doubts. And once an agent's relationship with his control has been corrupted it becomes useless.'

I hesitate. 'Then why didn't Mossad just dump Jacob in the harbour? It's happened before.'

He frowns. 'Watkins had given Mossad a reason to suspect the CIA were involved, and the Israelis couldn't afford to upset the Americans at that time.' He pauses again and his face relaxes. 'No. It happened just as Watkins had imagined it would. Mossad decided to retire Jacob and set him up in a nice little coffee house in Cyprus. He was able to resign from the embassy by telling them his brother wanted help with the family business. The ambassador was sorry to see him go, of course, and gave him a generous retirement gift. And, since he wasn't dismissed, the embassy was able to pay him a pension entitlement.' He smiles. 'So, you see, everyone was happy. In fact, Jacob was a damn sight better off thanks to Watkins. The Lebanese would have rumbled him sooner or later.'

I release a breath. 'But what if Mossad hadn't taken the bait? They would have known we were onto Jacob and could have made it difficult for us to get rid of him without attracting unwanted attention.' I lean forward. 'It was risky.'

'Or romantic?' he responds. 'Anyway, it worked. You must have seen the file.'

'Yes. But what you've just told me wasn't on it.'

'No,' he agrees easily, 'that part stays on my file, I'm afraid.' Then, glancing down at the board and rubbing his hands together, he adds briskly, 'Now, how about this game?'

I push forward the king's pawn, followed by the king's bishop pawn, and catch the brief smile that crosses my companion's face. Is it pleasure or the scent of blood? I know I'm going to be slaughtered, but what the hell? The King's Gambit hasn't been played in the club for years. It's the least I can do in memory of old Watkins.

Sweet Freedom

Existence itself is surely a debate.

– Kierkegaard

Simon's feet rested peacefully on the pedals as he coasted past the public toilet where someone had daubed Sweet Freedom in bold letters on the front wall. The building had been aesthetically conceived, despite its mundane purpose, and the slogan seemed misplaced and curiously aggressive. But then again, thought Simon, as he spun on down the hill towards the centre of town, perhaps the meaning was biological rather than political.

Simon often worried about questions it might have been better to ignore. Perhaps this was a symptom of neurosis; an over-sensitised reaction to the twentieth century, or the dawn of a new-age, feminine man. Maybe it was just random genetic distribution. In any event, today, Simon gave the matter no more than a passing thought. It was Friday, with the weekend seductively in sight, soaring high above his bicycle like a graceful swallow.

Even Beth, imprisoned by the conviction that ironing shirts and casseroling lamb chops were doing little for the validation of her psyche, had been unable to dent his upbeat mood. 'You're getting marmalade on that book,' she had scolded a few moments earlier. 'Why don't you read the paper before work like everyone else?'

'I want to finish this chapter,' he'd replied reasonably and, because he felt good, fired back a question of his own: 'How do you know everyone else reads the paper at breakfast?'

'I bet no one reads *The Rise and Fall of the Roman Empire*.'

He sighed. 'I finished *Decline and Fall* yesterday. This one's about philosophy.'

'Philosophy?'

'Existentialism, actually.'

Beth's eggshell cracked loudly. 'What on earth would you know about existentialism, actually?'

'Not much,' he conceded, glancing at the ruins of her egg. 'That's why I'm reading the book.'

'Yes,' she persisted with heavy patience, 'but for what practical purpose?'

'Why should a purpose have to be practical?'

Noticing her expression, he added, 'Anyway, a knowledge of philosophy might be useful.'

'Useful?' The second egg was pulverised. 'How might it be useful?'

'I don't know.' He waved a hand vaguely. 'In my work perhaps?'

The shrill scream of laughter had unnerved him. Beth scraped splintered shell from a yellow pool of yolk. 'I wasn't aware the choice between leather or suede involved metaphysics.'

Simon collected his book and rose from the table with dignity. He had no intention of remaining a shoe salesman all his life. In fact, he hadn't wanted to be one in the first place but it was the only job on offer without leaving town. The employment officer had told him this was the worst recession for sixty years, and he was lucky to get anything. Simon had worked in the bookshop before it closed down, and wanted something that allowed time for reading. 'Try the library,' his ex-boss advised, with preoccupied irony, disinclined to waste time cutting his losses and getting out of town. The employment officer suggested a training course. 'Why?' Simon had replied. 'So I won't be able to find a better job?'

He gave Beth a farewell kiss, which she met with haste but not aversion, and mounted his bicycle without looking back.

Simon was a dreamer and a doubter. Doubt is good, but too much can cause paralysis. Simon's doubt was prodigious and ate time. It wasn't that he wasted time. It just dribbled away unnoticed, like air escaping from a slow puncture in one of his tyres.

From the age of seven, so the psychologists and Jesuits tell us, we begin to reason. Unless fortified by prejudice, arrogance and ignorance, at that moment we become victims of doubt. A gulf of doubt. This, in itself, is not a bad thing unless it becomes wide enough to undermine self-confidence and paralyse further development. Simon's gulf was of Grand Canyon dimensions. His doubt defined his existence. I doubt, therefore I am.

The painter, Paul Gauguin, was supposed to have said, apropos of something or other, possibly a cracked palette or a model with PMT, 'When one thinks about life, one dreams of revenge.' Simon found this observation entirely reasonable. His problem was identifying the person or persons responsible. Revenge requires a focus – a culprit, if you like, someone upon whom the blame falls squarely, without reservation. And the only person to fit the bill so far, disregarding – for complex reasons of youthful loyalty – God, his parents or the local scout master, was (rather depressingly) himself.

Entering the main street, he reflected sadly on the case against self-analysis. It seemed, for example, to be a matter of appalling injustice that those most in need of doubt were the ones blithely dismissive of it. 'Gawd save me from wishy-washy wankers,' a thick-necked, beer-gutted uncle had shouted at Simon's father one day during a family barbecue. 'You never know where you are with the bastards. Give me someone who can stick to his principles no matter what happens.' Simon's father, turning the sausages, had enquired mildly, 'Even when those principles are obviously wrong? Surely it's a sign of wisdom, rather than weakness, to modify your views in the light of new ideas?' But the beer-gutted uncle was unstoppable. 'Yeah, and never bloody well get round to doing anything!'

Simon padlocked his bike and rang the bell on the rear door of the shoe shop, feeling the confusion of genetic inheritance. Sic transit gloria mundi…Tuesday, Wednesday, Thursday, Friday. Leaving only the weekend to confront – from the sanctity of his reading chair – the improbable apotheosis of mankind.

'Running late again, are we?' The question came from a gangling youth with galloping acne, slicked down hair, and an astonished expression frozen permanently to his face. It was the store owner's son, Jeremy.

Simon brightened. 'You should be able to get here on time. You live upstairs.'

Jeremy sniffed. 'I'm not late. You are.'

Simon glanced at his watch. 'Actually, I'm forty-five seconds early.'

Jeremy consulted his own watch with a flourish. It was a flashy job that tourists are apt to regret buying on their first trip to Singapore, and told the time almost incidentally to a maze of miscellanea as irrelevant to most people as wind velocity in Swaziland, or noon temperature in the Amazon Basin.

'Actually,' observed Jeremy, full of misplaced pomp, 'you're two minutes and seventeen seconds late.'

'Get your old man to dock it from my pay,' Simon replied, moving to the front door to welcome early customers.

It was a better than average haul for a Friday. One small boy and a big, woolly dog. The boy silently thrust an envelope into Simon's hand and turned his attention to the dog. The envelope contained instructions and money from the boy's mother. He was to be fitted with new school shoes, given the change and sent off to class.

By the time this complicated transaction had been completed, business was plunging towards a mid-morning slump and Simon knew he would have to seek distraction by conversation with Jeremy. He opted for an opening gambit from an unfinished line commenced the previous day. 'It's still there,' he said, meaning the slogan on the toilet wall.

As expected, Jeremy rose to the occasion. With an elaborate gesture of relief he replied, 'I'm so glad.'

'I'm talking about the graffiti on the public loo. I told you about it yesterday.'

'And I told you yesterday that I don't read lavatory walls.'

'Ah well, perhaps you should. There are some very good ones nowadays. They're becoming a valid literary genre.'

Simon waited for the outburst but Jeremy continued polishing a silver shoe horn in contemplative silence.

Disappointed, Simon added, 'It happens to be on the outside wall. The one facing the street. I'd have thought even you'd have trouble missing that.'

This drew a response, but not the one Simon was hoping for.

'I happen to know,' replied Jeremy slowly, 'that there's nothing written on that wall.'

Simon's interest quickened. This was extraordinary. Surprise was not usually evident in Jeremy's personality.

'How do you know?'

'Because my uncle painted it on Wednesday.'

Simon considered the statement. He knew the slogan had been there since last Monday but was distracted by the news that Jeremy's uncle painted toilets.

'Perhaps he wrote it. You know, as a political statement or signature of some kind.'

'My uncle,' said Jeremy, aloof with unexpected calm, 'doesn't paint toilet walls. He tells other people when to paint them. He's on the town council.'

Of course, thought Simon, your family owns half the bloody town and controls the other half from the council floor. He said, 'Well, I suggest your uncle gets someone to look at the wall again.'

The discussion was aborted by a lunchtime rush in the shape of the postmistress bustling in for a new pair of winter boots.

When Jeremy returned from lunching at his Aunty's café further down the high street, he immediately challenged Simon. 'What are you up to now?'

Simon glanced up from the cardboard boxes. 'Unpacking this new line of brogues as you told me. Have you forgotten already?'

'I meant the toilet wall. There's nothing written there. I've just been up for a look.'

Simon hesitated, a brogue in each hand. Incredible, he thought. It couldn't have been repainted since this morning, could it? The thought was immediately followed by a worrying proposition that Jeremy might be turning the tables.

'So, I've driven you to the wall at last,' he said, trying to regain lost ground, but Jeremy was in no mood for jokes.

'This is just another one of your pathetic attempts to stir me up, isn't it?'

'What is?'

'When you told me you'd seen the writing on the…'

Jeremy's voice trailed away and Simon laughed, returning to the brogues. They didn't speak again all day.

Simon checked the toilet wall on the way home. Sweet Freedom, sang the bold white letters. Since it was highly unlikely that Jeremy had lied, Simon fell into a river of doubt. He decided to risk seeking advice from Beth.

'I have absolutely no interest in public toilets,' she advised, with a look that could have curdled milk, 'with or without graffiti.'

So Simon retired to the safety of his reading chair, finding the weekend existentially beyond reach. Unable to concentrate, he slept badly, waking at three in the morning with a sweeping rush of panic at the prospect of life, as we have constituted it, never reaching enlightenment, remaining untenable and irretrievably bizarre. Not wanting to wake Beth, he waited for the dawn alone. Consumed by doubt.

The following Monday, on the way to work, he saw the boy with the new school shoes bouncing a tennis ball against the toilet wall. Deciding on impulse to seek the company of a fellow traveller, Simon brought his bike to a clumsy halt and yelled, 'Can you read that wall?'

Interrupted, the boy took his eye off the ball which came back and struck him in the face. The ball rolled away and he scampered after it.

'Hey,' shouted Simon with a tone desperate enough to alarm the boy into stopping, 'what does that wall say?'

The boy stared at the big white letters and then back to Simon again.

Reality paused. A snapshot in time. Elsewhere children starved, rainforests diminished and wars flamed, but here the world was still, silent and at peace. Simon knew it all; in one imploded fragment he saw the big picture – time and space and what it meant to be here rather than there, now rather than then, and why the questions were always bigger than the answers. He stood before it like a man in front of a firing squad at the instant the triggers are squeezed. His concentration was sublime and when the judgement came he didn't flinch.

'It don't say nothing,' called the boy and spun on his heel, forgetting the tennis ball as he began to run; putting as much distance as he could between himself and the sort of stranger his mother constantly warned him about.

During the lunch break, Simon went next door to the hardware store and purchased a can of white spray paint from Jeremy's cousin. Riding home after work, he paused to confront the wall again, carefully tracing over each letter and stepping back to admire the result. Sweet Freedom, it stated reassuringly.

'There,' he said to himself with grim satisfaction. 'Let them deny it now.'

Remounting his bicycle, he noticed the police car.

Beth's reaction to his loss of job was unexpected. 'It's lucky the council wants me back,' she said, glancing at her watch and rustling the morning paper. 'I've just got time for an egg.'

Simon approached the stove and warily selected a saucepan. 'I might do a course at college,' he said, boiling the water. 'You know, creative cooking for existentialists or something.'

'Yes, dear,' said Beth, without looking up from the finance pages. 'Whatever keeps you out of trouble.'

Simon watched her through the window as she left, the smart new skirt swinging jauntily and high heels clicking on the garden path. There was no mistaking the confident stride. It seemed curiously familiar. Like something he had read recently.

A Collapsible Paradise

> If by eternity is understood not endless temporal duration but timelessness, then he lives eternally who lives in the present.
>
> – Wittgenstein

Sometimes, without warning, she would regard him seriously and ask, 'Why don't you surprise me?'

'How?' he would enquire reasonably, glancing up from whatever he was doing.

'Oh, I don't know. It doesn't matter how. Just surprise me, for Christ's sake!'

And then he would watch her for a moment, as a dog might watch a loved master uncertain of a command, before his eyes flickered away with a hint of something she took to be guilt, and a well-worn, if not weary, silence fell across them again.

God, she thought one day as the now familiar panic spiralled through her body, I'm going mad just waiting for something to happen. So she consulted the university's psychology department, partly to convince herself she wasn't going mad, but more importantly to discover if it were possible to *surprise* surprise.

'Do you love him?'

'Yes.'

'And he loves you?'

'Yes.'

'How do you know?'

'Sorry?'

'How do you know he loves you?'

The question set her back; literally. She felt her body being thrust into the chair as if she had just taken off on a plane. She bailed out.

'How do I know the sky is blue,' she said. But then, reading the look in his eyes as he sat behind the authoritative safety of his book-laden desk, she relented, adding, 'I don't know. It's like religious faith, I guess. Is it possible for anyone to be absolutely certain they're loved?'

He smiled and some of the tension in the small room evaporated. 'People like to think so.' He pushed a hand under his glasses. The movement suggested boredom or weariness and she wondered how often he'd heard the story before. He readjusted the glasses, met her eyes and finished the statement. 'But most remain doubtful all their lives, despite managing highly successful relationships.'

'Well,' she said with sudden conviction, 'I don't know.'

'You don't know if he loves you?'

'No! I know that. I just don't know how I know.'

He made no reply, and she listened to the currawongs on the lawn outside his window and glanced at the room. It was disappointing. A couple of indifferent prints, an impossibly overcrowded bookcase and a large pinboard scattered with schedules, newspaper clippings and a few photographs. One caught her eye. It was a woman with two small children and a large dog.

'Can you imagine life without him?'

She dragged her attention back to the desk. 'If I try hard enough.'

'And how does it look?'

'Uncomfortable.'

'In what way?'

She crossed her legs and adjusted the slim skirt. It was too early for a major confession; such as the possibility that she enjoyed being intellectually superior, so she opted for a safer road. 'We married young. I had never – in the Biblical sense – known anyone else.'

He nodded. 'Does he know you're here?'

'Yes,' she replied quickly, thinking, But not why I am here.

He made a note on a pad and asked, without looking up, 'Is the sexual part of the relationship okay?'

'Yes.'

He continued writing for a moment and then leant back. 'Let's summarise, shall we? You live in a healthy and apparently loving environment with your husband and young daughter. You have the freedom, and financial independence, to pursue your own interests – such as a degree in English literature at this university – without guilt or anxiety.' He paused, glanced at the pad, then placed his hands behind his head. 'As for surprise, it's like happiness. It happens as a result of something else, not as an end in itself. You can't place it on order. That's a contradiction in terms.' He smiled. 'I don't want to patronise, but you must be aware that you're an attractive, intelligent woman. Most people would envy you.' He gave a low, throaty chuckle. 'Some might even see your world as a kind of paradise.'

Her naked body arched in a hot, tense curve, like the video image lingering in her mind's eye. He was moving inside her with long, steady strokes, and she drew him deeper as the tempo increased. His mouth closed on an upright nipple before seeking her neck in a final, breathy rush. She clung to him but he rolled away, whispering, 'Jesus, that went off like a kangaroo dog at a butcher's picnic.'

'If that's a compliment,' she said, without turning her head, 'I'm glad you enjoyed it.'

His hand touched her face. 'Didn't you?'

She bit one of his fingers playfully. 'I was still thinking of that stupid film.'

'Well, you wanted a surprise.'

'Not a porn movie, for God's sake.'

He pushed himself up on one shoulder and gently traced a circle with his finger round a still firm nipple. 'That was tame. You should see some of the real stuff.'

'No thanks. But, as a matter of incidental interest, where have you seen it?'

He lay back on the pillow and she sensed his embarrassment. 'One of the blokes in the office had some.' He laughed uneasily at the memory.

'We screened it on the company video one night after work. Bloody rubbish, of course, but good for a laugh.'

'The woman's movement might not agree with you.'

He tweaked a nipple between finger and thumb. 'I like women who move.'

After a few moments of silence she selected a book from a stack on the floor, and he set the clock radio for the morning. Then, turning on his side, he faced her. 'What do you get from all those books?'

'An improved mind.'

'What's wrong with the one you've got?'

'Nothing.' She glanced at him and smiled. 'But there's always room for improvement.'

'Is that a dig at me?'

She sighed. 'Go to sleep, darling. I need to read this for a morning tutorial.'

He closed his eyes. 'What did the doctor have to say?'

'Doctor?'

'I thought you saw someone today?'

'He's not a doctor, for Christ's sake. He's a student counsellor at the uni.'

He opened his eyes. 'Well, what did he say?'

She reached across and touched his hair, drawing her fingers over an ear and gently pulling the lobe. 'He said I was living in paradise.'

The steady rush of the air conditioner and a chunk of blue sky glimpsed through the window conspired to spirit her away on a plane, ten thousand metres high and heading for a distant city where a car would be waiting…

' – you might achieve the opposite effect.'

She returned to the small room with a bump. 'Sorry?'

He was about forty, dressed with elegant casualness in faded corduroy jacket, washed-out jeans and desert boots. He slid off the front of his desk and walked back to the chair. 'I was pointing out that he might surprise you unpleasantly.'

She frowned. 'Why would he do that?'

He smiled. 'I don't suppose he'd do it intentionally. But if you keep insisting on surprise the results may not be to your liking. Suppose he took up weasel desexing, for example.'

She straightened in the chair. 'I wasn't thinking of that sort of surprise.'

He pushed a hand under his glasses. 'I know you weren't.' He closed his eyes, squeezing a finger and thumb against each lid as if to keep them shut. 'Suppose you give me an example of the sort of surprise you were thinking of.'

She'd anticipated the question, of course, but had no answer. She looked away. Her chair was in a slightly different position from the previous visit and she could see the woman in the photograph clearly. She was dark-skinned, but whether from pigment or tan was uncertain. She had a pleasantly peaceful face that somehow managed to catch a balance between compliance and independence. Her hands rested with quiet possession on the shoulders of the two children and she seemed content, not smug, but self-contained, as if she didn't need anyone, but wouldn't shut people out either.

She turned back to the desk and found him watching her. To her horror, she felt a sting of tears and sniffed like a bewildered schoolgirl. He pushed a box of tissues across the desk and she grabbed one angrily.

'Perhaps some women might envy me,' she said brokenly, and then paused, thinking of the face in the photograph. No. Not her. She doesn't envy anyone. 'But there must be something else.'

He placed his elbows on the desk forming a steeple with his hands beneath the chin. 'Let me tell you a secret. There's a fundamental core of boredom at the centre of all our lives, no matter how complex or exciting they may appear to the outsider. Where the intelligent person has an edge is that they can dismantle the unwanted scenario and rebuild it. A collapsible paradise. Not in a physical or geographical sense, but up here.' He tapped his temple. 'Happiness is mostly a point of view.'

She gave a disbelieving giggle. 'You mean invent things, like Walter Mitty?'

He smiled. 'There's nothing wrong with the occasional fantasy, but I'm not advocating is as a lifelong focus. I'm merely asking you to redefine reality.'

She considered the statement. 'Will it increase my chance of surprise?'

'Maybe. But remember, you can't place surprise on order. It doesn't work that way. It's like demanding that someone be spontaneous. Relax. Enjoy yourself, take life as it comes and climb a mountain now and then.'

The trouble with mountains, she thought as she parked the car and realised she was going to be late for the lecture, is that they are often hidden by cloud. Breathless from the sprint, she slumped into a seat at the rear of the lecture hall.

'Voltaire tells us life becomes bearable only when we remain in our own garden, minding our own business. But is this possible for the enquiring mind? Intelligence places us in jeopardy. Intellectually, emotionally and socially, the intelligent person is tormented by curiosity and sensitivity.' The lecturer's voice carried well in the almost empty hall. He was tall, thin and tense, with an unkempt beard below a prematurely bald head, making it seem – from where she sat – that his face was upside down. He kept rubbing a hand over the top of his head, as if checking for miraculous growth, and striking the lectern with karate blows to punctuate a phrase. 'In this sense, at least, the uneducated, the dull, and the unimaginative are the lucky ones, since they are spared this torment…'

She walked slowly back to the car tormented by what she hoped was heightened sensitivity.

That weekend, while descending from a mutual mountain, he came off his skis at high speed and broke a leg.

Entering the hospital ward, she managed to resist a smile at his discomfort. Perhaps, she thought, placing a bag of grapes on the bedside table, the dull and unimaginative don't entirely miss their share of torment. Smiling, she asked, 'How are you, darling?'

'I've known better moments.'

'That slope was difficult. Perhaps we should have stayed on the beginners' run.'

He shifted his weight and winced. 'Perhaps we should have stayed at home.'

She touched his arm. 'We were climbing a mountain together.'

He looked at her in that silent, worrying way she knew so well, and then began to eat the grapes.

She noticed the photograph was missing at once, but was unprepared for the way it seemed to change things.

She asked, 'Do you think ignorance is bliss?'

He smiled. 'There's little doubt that intelligence increases your capacity for pain, but it also gives greater scope for pleasure.' He paused. 'Any luck with the surprise crusade?'

'I'm adopting fatalism as a coping mechanism. From now on, I'm only worrying about keeping the chablis chilled and making sure I've got a fresh lemon to squeeze on the oysters.' She looked away. 'There's no sense rocking a boat unless you want to sink it.'

'What happens if someone does something you disapprove?'

'I'll show them they're wrong.'

'By argument?'

'By example.'

'And if they chose to ignore your example? After all, it's possible you might be wrong.'

She hesitated. 'It's possible. But I'd never knowingly expect anyone I loved to do something I wasn't prepared to do myself.'

'Ah, yes. The escape clause. Knowingly.' He repeated the word softly, almost to himself, and she met his eyes, suddenly fearful.

'What happened to the photograph?'

He blinked a couple of times and glanced at the board. 'I threw it away.'

'Why?

He shrugged. 'It was no longer part of my life.'

She felt the familiar sting of tears and he pushed the tissues towards her. She grabbed one and dabbed her eyes. The image of the pleasant looking, dark-skinned woman, two children and the big dog, was as vivid as if their photo was still pinned to the board. 'This is stupid,' she said, 'I don't even know why I'm crying.'

She heard the front door slam as she lay on the sofa reading.

'Hi, Mum,' called her daughter, heading for the kitchen. Moments later, the girl stood in the doorway clutching a clumsy sandwich, pigtails awry and school tunic rumpled. 'Whatya reading?'

'*Candide*.'

'Who?'

'*Candide*. By Voltaire.'

'Volt who?'

'Don't they teach you anything at that school? We pay them enough money.'

The girl munched thoughtfully. 'They don't teach us about volts.' She brightened. 'The teachers are pretty dumb, though.'

'This has nothing to do with electricity, darling. It's about a search for happiness.'

'Sounds like a drag. Can I watch TV?'

'Not in here.' She looked up but her daughter had gone. 'And don't forget your homework.'

She stretched and dozed. Then the front door slammed again and he was there, briefcase and newspaper tucked neatly under his arm.

She sat up and glanced at her watch. 'Good God! Is that the time?'

'It must be a bloody good book.'

'It's Voltaire's *Candide*.'

'Whose what?'

She stood up and smiled. 'Don't you start.' She touched his arm but he turned away. 'Is anything wrong?'

He glanced back. 'Why should anything be wrong?'

'No reason.'

He looked at her in silence for a moment. 'As a matter of fact, something's right.' He paused and she waited, afraid to speak. 'I've been promoted. It'll involve an interstate transfer. They want me there quickly.'

Her throat tightened. 'How soon?'

'The end of the month. I'll have to arrange accommodation – '

'What about the house?'

He hesitated. 'Don't worry. I think you should have it.' He turned away again. 'You'll be fine.'

'And our daughter?'

'She belongs here, of course. She's much more like you than me.' He smiled and tapped his forehead. 'Brainy. You don't need me. You've been telling me that for a long time – '

'I haven't!'

He met her eyes with a confidence she hadn't seen for years. 'Yes, you have. You're so self-sufficient. You don't need me. I doubt you need anyone, really, except perhaps Voltaire.'

'But what about you?' she said quickly. 'You need...' Her voice tapered away. '...someone.'

He took a deep breath. 'And I've found someone. She was a nurse at the hospital. I don't know how she has time for me. She's already got two children and a damn great dog.' He smiled, as if relieved of some burden. 'I'm glad you haven't started dinner. We're going out to celebrate the promotion. She's looking forward to the move.' He turned away. 'I've just got time for a quick shower.'

She sank back to the sofa. Reality had slowed, like a frozen video image advancing frame by frame. She sat straight and stiff, the paperback Voltaire hugged to her breasts. And was still there, in exactly the same position, when the front door closed as he left.

The Square Cut

Ryan Curtis knew his Foreign Service career was marooned on a plateau that beckoned retirement unless disturbed by the forces of improbability. His last two postings had remained pegged at First Secretary level, and now – although this seemed to annoy Alice, his wife, far more than himself – a Head of Mission appointment seemed to have slipped beyond reach. So when the executive suite summons came before morning tea on a slow Wednesday, it caused a flutter of nervous excitement unknown since receiving news of his first posting more than twenty years earlier.

Departmental Secretary, Duncan MacDonald, gazed reflectively at the window. 'The Cold War evokes nostalgia when placed alongside the chaos of global terrorism,' he was saying. 'Things were mostly black and white back then – big picture, them and us and bugger the rest – but now there are so many tinpot conflict permutations, it's hard to know who the real villains are.' He paused to glance back at Ryan, seated stiffly in a visitor's chair and trying hard to look comfortable.

'Back then,' the Secretary continued, 'it was easier to draw distinctions between diplomacy and espionage. Now, the issue is not so clear cut. The threat to world order doesn't always come from political, national or military considerations. It tends to be up here.' He tapped his temple. 'In the mind.' He gave a slow, knowing smile. 'The increasing polarisation of belief.' He leant back in the chair and regarded Ryan with a steady gaze. 'We're in danger of being driven back to the Middle Ages by the kind of fundamentalism that threw Saladin against Richard the Lionheart.'

MacDonald removed a sheet of paper from a folder marked Top Secret and slid it across the desk. 'Off the record, of course, but it represents the gist of our current thinking.'

Ryan knew the rumours, and glanced quickly down the page. 'It's interesting, but I really don't see what it has to do with me.'

'Don't be disingenuous, Ryan.'

Ryan shrugged. 'I have no special interest or qualification. There must be others – '

'But none with a square cut like yours.'

Ryan hesitated. MacDonald enjoyed a certain eccentricity among senior colleagues, but surely the last remark had been misheard?

'Sorry?'

'The square cut you played off old Singh last Sunday. Final over before tea. It told me more about you than your personal file ever could.'

Ryan drew a slow breath. 'Are you saying I'm being offered this post because I happened to hit a four at a social cricket match against the Indian High Commissioner's eleven?'

The Secretary smiled. 'Perhaps.'

'But that's preposterous!'

'Is it?'

Ryan hesitated. Perhaps this was some kind of test. 'Isn't it?'

MacDonald folded his hands over a flat stomach and settled back in the chair. 'Let's put false modesty aside, Ryan. You know your recent work with the Pacific Regional Security Committee has been highly regarded. You'd be a contender even without the square cut.' He paused and tugged an earlobe. 'You may not be aware that I'm a serious student of cricket. Of course, I've played the game since early childhood, but during university I began to study it as well. As a means of psychological and intellectual assessment. I've found it rewarding, and usually accurate.'

'But one shot,' Ryan protested, 'a fluke. I haven't played regularly for years. It was sheer luck the ball came off the middle of the bat.'

MacDonald waved a hand dismissively. 'I was at the other end, remember? Only the bowler, and possibly the umpire, had a better view.' He leant forward and lowered his voice. 'Let me tell you what I saw.' He paused and Ryan waited in a state of suspended disbelief as MacDonald warmed to his theme. 'You had already taken a couple of painful blows in that over. You could have closed up shop.' He allowed himself an avuncular smile. 'After all, you had an experienced player at the other end, and it was almost tea. But when that ball rose outside the off stump, going away – Singh does manage a quite respectable outswinger – you struck one of the finest square cuts I've seen at that level of cricket for many years.'

'A fluke,' Ryan repeated faintly, looking away, as if seeking escape. 'I hit it without thinking: in anger, perhaps.'

'That's possible,' conceded MacDonald reasonably. 'An instinctive reaction to having been struck by the previous ball.' He waited until Ryan's gaze returned to meet his own, and added softly, 'But it wasn't. The Secretary's voice took on a new, and curiously sinister, tone. 'Shall I tell you what it really was? That square cut of yours.'

Ryan moved his head in a barely perceptible nod.

'It was a confirmation of intellect, through judgement, timing and precision.'

Ryan waited, spellbound, as MacDonald continued. 'If you had acted in anger, what do you suppose the odds would have been against the ball meeting the middle of your bat, going to ground as it did, before bisecting the gap between gully and point?'

Ryan shook his head, unable to speak.

'A hundred to one? A thousand to one?'

Ryan became aware of a sense of resignation. Perhaps Duncan needed a rest? Was this an early stage of stress-induced breakdown?

'No,' said MacDonald firmly, as if reading Ryan's thoughts. 'Hitting the ball the way you did required analysis not anger. Precision not panic. To move the back foot away from the flight, keep the head still, balance the body and roll the wrists at exactly the right instant, involved a singular quality.' He paused. 'A quality I require if my department is going into bat against terrorism.'

In the hollow silence following this statement, Ryan heard only the slow release of his own breath. Why not, he thought. If I edge this one through to the keeper, there will be no disgrace. Merely a chance to renovate the coast cottage a few years earlier. But if it comes off the middle and reaches the boundary…who knows? Perhaps the Head of Mission posting Alice so passionately desires. He swung back to face the Secretary. 'I'll take it, he said.

'Splendid!' MacDonald stood up and shook Ryan's hand. 'I knew you were our man. Give me a day or so to get our people on the same page as their people, and maybe we can tee up a briefing schedule for next week.'

Outside, Ryan glanced along the carpeted corridor to make sure he was alone, before playing an imaginary square cut. He kept his head still, moved his feet and rolled the wrists. But somehow it wasn't the same. This one lacked the spontaneous conviction of the first.

Poems

Evening at Murunna Point

The grassy twilight deepens
on the hill above the bay;
the sea is dark and washed by cloud
in the haunting of the day.

Gulaga broods against the sky,
a tapestry of light,
her green and darkling shadows
beckoning the night.

On the lake a blue crane wades
with sad and secret grace,
treading the sandbars of a dream
inside some distant place.

A moment caught by beauty drawn
from byways strange and still,
no vanity disturbs this peace
on the path across the hill.

Epiphany

First light dusts the bedroom wall,
and somewhere in the garden a bird lifts me
with the careful vigour of its song:
clear and fluted, like a rising passion,
that cracks against the air and dies.
A whipbird, his jaunty crest
dancing the tangled hedges
by the possum-scarred gum tree.
Where the brash and busy wattle birds
chase with darting wings.

I take my cup of black, unsweetened tea,
to a sheltering deck behind the house;
grey boards dappled by the willow,
and trailing honeysuckle haunted
by a sudden memory of flowers.
The air is cool. And cathedral-still.
No human sound desecrates its silence.

A bright wedge of Wallaga Lake glimmers
between the branches of a plum tree
and the white magnolia. Pelicans drift
upon the tide like ghostly and forgotten sails,
as if towards a sea that you and I once knew.
And loved with all the careless hope
of yesterday.

I rest upon the wicker sofa with its broken
strands, and cushions which you stitched
so long ago, and try to remember where
it all began: this fractured and malignant light;
this aspect of a ruined life.
This desolated time. Its stolen sleep
falling from my eyes like scales.
In the prison cell of a tyrant,
where the unshaded bulb of consciousness
can never be switched off.
And birdsong is unknown.

The Apple Tree

In that other country of the past,
there is a farm,
abandoned as a result of unrecorded tragedy,
and rambling into weed-haunted wasteland,
where wild creatures roam,
and claim sanctuary to raise their young.
It's a far and lonely place,
on the edge of an old forest,
where few people have any cause to visit.
Behind the farm, and pressing hard
against the trees,
as if trying to escape some large
but nameless cruelty,
is a long-neglected orchard full of apples,
betrayed by market forces and forgotten.
Apples with elegant and graceful-sounding names:
Egremont Russets, D'Arcy Spice, Lord Lambourne,
and the Beauty of Bath.
They're lost and gone forever now,
like street kids shooting drugs,
their gangling growth unpruned,
and fruit rotting where it falls.

In the middle of the orchard
stands the highest tree, thick-stemmed
and twisted with age.
But still bearing the sweetest fruit:
glowing in the dusk
like tiny crucibles of fire.
In scattered dreams, which may
or may not reflect reality,
I scramble through a broken fence
after school and munch on apples
like some contented beast
ignorant of its guilt.
Then I climb the highest tree,
right to the very top,
and rest in a cradle of sheltering leaves.
From where I can see the farmhouse roof…
and a curl of smoke from one of its chimneys.
The place has been empty for years,
and my flesh tightens under a knife edge
of sudden fear,
causing the tree to shiver around me,
as if disturbed by beating wings.
But I'm well hidden, I tell myself;
is it possible anyone can know
that I am here?

Below me, the tops of smaller trees
stretch away like the surface
of a rippling field of wheat.
Empty and silent.
Except for the soft thud of a wary footstep,
that drags my gaze downwards like a startled bird.
But it's just a falling clutch of over-ripe apples,
coming to rest among dappled grasses
as winter moons on frozen and forgotten seas.
I look up again and, to the east,
the forest darkens
into silhouette and shadow.
And to the west, beyond the farmhouse roof,
with its unexplained ribbon of grey smoke,
a big, yellow sun is masked by vaporous cloud.
Giving off the tawny sheen of sweet water
running down through honey.
I catch my breath,
sensing the closeness of unknowable things.
Feeling them move around me,
like the folds of a dark and voluptuous cloak.
Whose touch is gentle,
yet as strong as a discovered poem,
or a picture,
or a piece of music,
that makes you feel as tall as Christ,
even though you don't know why.

I gaze beyond the farmhouse roof,
towards the horizon,
like an eagle watching for its mate,
and a sudden coldness falls upon me,
as the future dreams me into life.
I can feel it breathing:
all around me in the air,
as if coming from the apple tree itself.
And I am born at the age of twelve,
seven metres high above the ground,
cradled by a tree that nobody wants,
and watched by an empty farmhouse with its chimney
of culpable smoke.

I climb back down,
to a world that looks unchanged
but will never be the same again.
And neither will I.

The Cliff Path – Then and Now

But at my back I always hear
Time's winged chariot hurrying near.
– Andrew Marvell

Captured by a searching sea,
the child runs,
as if carried by the wind,
headlong down a low, rambling cliff,
through trees haunted
by the rasp
of pebbles feeding on the tide.
Leaping the sun-baked rifts
of winter's sinuous clay,
stumbling, breathless and giddy,
and rushing on,
swept up by the sense
of being two people;
one travelling faster than the other.
Head and shoulders
pulling the slower feet
of someone else.
Someone lost within the perfect joy
of running so fast,
he cannot catch himself.

*

Now, a senior citizen of sorts,
but disinclined for its diversions,
he moves to strike a tennis ball,
while coming to the net,
or walk the afternoon away
into the evening edges
of a different sea.
The long land brooding
with its short history
of a closer past.
And sometimes with the light upon the cusp,
that fleeting moment when the world is true,
he sees the child,
ahead of him on the path,
running at the distance
like a shadow from the sun.
And glancing backwards
into his future;
as if afraid
of being caught.

Counting Spoons in the Age of Trump

The louder he talked of his honour the faster we counted our spoons.
– Ralph Waldo Emerson (1803–1882)

Trapped inside revolving doors
adrift in cyberspace,
with psychedelic petits fours
and egg upon our face,
in painted dreams of bright redemption
we scan for silver moons;
echoing the blind convention
of counting stolen spoons.
Such detail as the eyes can see
(when they're engaged to look)
is drawn towards conspiracy
to bait a Janus hook
with urban myth and half-baked lies,
ignorance, fear and hate,
to suffer fools but scorn the wise,
by tweeting God is great!

On Being Lucky

Further along the dinner table
the talk is of hospitals and operations.
Of how one of us has been placed
under the surgeon's knife.
The woman at my elbow
inclines herself in my direction,
as if sharing something valuable,
and whispers, 'Doesn't that make you
realise how lucky you are?'
I turn away, knowing she is waiting
for my nod of affirmation;
for words that might release the empty weight of
consolation. 'You're right,' she wants to hear me say,
'I am lucky. Clinical depression is nothing compared
to having your chest sliced open by a razor.'

The evening ends and car doors slam,
as invisible guests carol their goodbyes.
I pause on the way out,
feeling the sting of midnight
make the first of a thousand cuts.
Each one unseen,
and sharper than the last.

Asking for Trouble

For where is here?
And when is now?
And how are things to be?
For why is this?
And who is that?
And what will set me free?

For this is how things really are
How thinking makes them so
When the sky has lost its colour
And there's nowhere else to go.

For I have seen eternity
And borne its midnight brand
On endless days repeated
In a single grain of sand
I have crossed its lonely desert
And sailed its frozen sea
I have lingered where the winter dark
Has cast its eye on me.

And all I ever wanted
Was honey still for tea
Honey still for tea.

The Girl on the Railway Platform

Alone with the sting of constant stress,
and already defeated
by a short and brutal life,
she struggles to control two young children.
Her face, once pretty, is pinched and defensive.
Her eyes, once friendly and wide,
are narrow and sly. She moves with the wariness
of a caged animal; trapped by a system
that says she is responsible
for things she doesn't understand.

Although herself little more than a child,
she's a mother now, and her innocence
(which she doesn't care to think about)
is long gone; a starship flight away.
But it's not just disenchantment,
no, it's something worse than that,
far worse, something almost sinister.

As I watch, she catches my eye
with what seems like a brief
and silent plea for help.
But instantly it's gone, and suspicion sets in.
You're part of it, I see her thinking,
you, and your well-dressed wife.
Going into town with money in your pockets.
She looks away, and I know she's found it necessary
to cheat the system in order to survive.

In her world, honesty is a sign of weakness.
In her world, relationships are traded
for the best possible return,
like any other commodity.
In her world, there is no music,
no art, no books, no poetry to embalm the pain.
She's alone and trapped and doesn't know why.
It's all there; the process is etched
into her skin like a concentration camp symbol.
It's shot through her body
and comes to the surface
in the downward slant of her mouth,
the slump of her shoulders,
and the raw, defeated look in her eyes.
She's been betrayed by life,
and banished to an underworld
without compassion,
where nobody cares what happens to her.
And she doesn't know who to blame.
That's the nub of it, really;
there is no one…
except, perhaps, all of us.

Goblins

Twenty metres away,
at eye level above the path,
something hovers on the air,
painted by the brushstrokes
of a setting sun,
and spinning inside the hollow flame of mystery.

It's a leaf,
trapped between two invisible membranes
of a spider's web,
and twisting
with the flickering shape of something else.
Something on the edge of fear,
seen dimly, before the dawn,
like a child's bedtime story, unexplained.

But that first cold and rushing moment,
before knowing what it really was,
became part of a world
long since abandoned.
A world of magic spells and witches,
and dragons off the edge of the map.
A world without reason, rationality or science.
Where things are clothed with the wonder
of heaven and hell.
And goblins all around.

The Boundary Rider

In lonely watches of the night,
he passes by in smothered light.
Gleaming with all passion spent,
in promises unkept but meant.

And distant echoes of repent.

The muffled door and creaking stair,
are torn from nightmares cradled there.
This is how our great world ends:
with dreams and sins and absent friends.

And desperate hopes to make amends.

Annie Dreaming

Unknown ghosts are by her bed,
whispering memories in her head.
Pleasures innocent of earthly sin,
cast shadows of what might have been.

Shapes of beauty lost and deep,
nibble at the edge of sleep.
When morning comes she wakes and finds,
regretful day behind the blinds.

As seasons change and kinships call,
and when her face turns to the wall;
there'll be no song that's worth redeeming,
half as sweet as Annie dreaming.

Blessed Is the Fruit

(For the memory of my mother)

Hollow-eyed and midnight-pale, she hesitates
for reasons vastly unexplained.
The thin call quickening one of us
to her bedside.
'Who is that?' she asks,
moving her head in tiny validation
of our birth.
Then falls away again, towards
the echoing abyss of delirium.
'She will not pass the night,'
the doctor says, hurrying
with his stethoscope at the door.
The priest arrives, and round her bed
in clumsy, half-circled vigil,
we seek comfort in the chant
of meaningless refrain.
Afterwards, he tells her, 'Now you may sleep.'
To which she replies with sudden voice,
'And make sure I'm truly asleep
before they roast me.'
I glance at the priest, and on his lips
the fleeting smile
seduces a non-believer
into prayer.

Meeting Mary

The year was green and wonder seen
in every place to dwell.
But life ran deep with the unquiet sleep
of love's untasted well.

The day we met time lingered yet
in a glow of childhood truth,
and on her breast did gently rest
the innocence of youth.

Her eyes burned bright with wondrous light,
her step a vibrant thing,
and her hair spun dark with the shining mark
of a raven's midnight wing.

The world spins by, the seasons die,
and winter holds the line,
but that first day, so far away,
still tastes of summer wine.

Sonnet for Wallaga Lake

For Tony and Kris

Who keeps a vigil by this lake
in sorrow or for any sake?
As forests brood with sacred sound,
in whispered prayers on Holy ground,
and evening shadows calmly grace
Mount Gulaga's ancient Dreamtime face.
Who writes her story for the stage
of history's reconstructed page?
Or seeks redemption for the crime
of such arrogantly wasted time?
While flags of malice are unfurled
on the chaos of a shackled world,
and costs are counted where they lay –
beyond the reach of judgement day.

Who keeps a vigil by this lake
for reconciliation's sake?
Who finds solace in a place
that offers hope within its grace?

Imagination

There is no shape, no closing wall,
no boundary fence to ride.
Its kingdom is that other world
where Gods are said to stride.

A fabled place of magic sails
that release our earthly tie,
and lift us high above the clouds
where we begin to fly.

Oh, flights of fearless fancy!
Such wondrous, soaring things.
How sweet it is to drift aloft
on a dreaming beat of wings!

To step inside a moment
that resonates with blue,
and there beside the endless sky,
come face to face with you.

The image of perfection;
the beauty of your birth.
To catch a glimpse of paradise,
before falling back to earth.

The Taste of Rainbows

For what becomes of innocence
worn down and lost in life?
The happy doubt of painful youth,
the calm and tempered strife.

The cosiness of winter dark,
the fey, unravelled thing;
the creative expectation
unanswered questions bring.

The universe is held aloft;
its mysteries lay unfurled,
but the night stars still outnumber
all the sand grains of the world.

And in the deepest mystery,
beyond microscopic reach,
rests the rainbow taste of wisdom
no scientist can teach.

And that's the way it should be;
untouchable and still,
with nothing but the shadow
of a light upon the hill.

Adelaide, 2 July 2016

For Stephen Matthews and Brenda Eldridge

Talking about poetry in a public library
on Election Day is unlikely to make
much happen in a crowded,
confusing and corrupted world.

But consolation against the odds
invites solace and empathy, which –
reflected in a prism of the moment –
seeks a foothold in the quicksand of existence.

We are what we are: chemistry made conscious
by a cosmic convulsion beyond invention;
molecules of light, beading the surface of infinity –
searching, always searching, for the centre.

On Federal Election Day, 2016, I spoke at a forum on poetry, as part of the twentieth birthday celebrations for Ginninderra Press.

Breakfast after Paris, 14 November 2015

For Toby and Jasper

Leave the pillow and come to the window
Two blackbirds are dancing the lawn
The sunlight is weaving the willow
With a weary old chance to be born.

To imagine a world – if just briefly –
Where yesterday's flickering hate
Was merely some digital nightmare
Escaped through the bars of its gate.

We pause over breakfast in kinship
With a child-painted card to redeem
Two generations of innocent faces
Held still in the arms of a dream.

Has the genie escaped from its bottle?
Will the madness of war simply grow?
How can God be so great in such evil?
When the face of a child says NO!

The Lost City of Aleppo, November 2016

A brooding mass of rubble
A hymn to futile rage
Aleppo rests in ruins
A footnote from a page
Torn from human chaos
And locked within its cage
Like a thought inside a bubble
Seeking to engage
The blinded eye of violence
Twisted lies and holy reeds
With a frightful silence
Among the withered seeds
Being counted out in limbo
On a string of Satan's beads.

The Ballad of Rachel's War

There was a day when she might sing
the bleakest winter into spring,
or weave a magic summer's lease
from autumn's tragic golden fleece.
That time back then – how long ago?
the twilight blue as liquid snow –
the beat of war upon her face,
her shoulders draped in victim's lace.
He was drift wood on the sand;
his memory lost in foreign land.
She sang for him her one last song –
a song of love a lifetime long.
But then the dark invading sea,
captured their tranquillity,
and Rachel saw a shadow there,
painted on the sunless air.
And now each day she takes a flower,
and stands before his silent bower.
The sculptured stone is smooth and cold,
but on its face her words are told:
I sang for you my one last song:
a song of love – a lifetime long.

String Theory

For Tim Metcalf

Hiawatha and Senacharib
Meet one night for a beer
Wanting to say in a relative way
How nice it is to be here
But this cannot be as we all can see
For if they were both in the house
Like the King with his string
They would always be – existentially –
somewhere else.

Terror Nebulous

For the first Australians

Caught on the unforgiving cusp
of a conqueror's perception,
in light from a star that no longer exists,
they become visible only in the accretion
of small things. For which there are no words.

They blink at the millennium;
with its dysfunctional shapes
of reconciliation and regret.
And quietly drown in the shadows
of a reconstructed history.

Waiting for their indigenous Godot.

Listening for the ticking
of his ancient blood.
In a story so endlessly untold,
even Beckett would have baulked
at the prospect.

Resurrection

For you and I
Must chase the sky
Beyond the point
Where eagles fly
From here and now
To there and then
As once it was –
And may be again
For lost inside
An endless wave
Like shadows
Haunting Plato's Cave
Our journey ends
Where it begins –
Free from ego
And the sins.

A Theory of Money

Everything is about money,
and money is about everything.
The real reason the political right and left
regard each other with so much odium
is because the right thinks the left
will steal its money, and the left
assumes the right already has. That's the shabby
truth about politics. Money. The nasty
little threadbare nub of ideological realism.
Forget justice, compassion and truth;
forget racism, poverty and traumatised
refugees; forget education and health.
Forget the forests and global warming.
It's all about money.
A vote-winning pitch inevitably
begins and ends with economic management,
because voters worrying about money
are less likely to notice the lies.
All is vanity. Indeed.
But vanity is also about money.

The Philistines

They watch commercial TV,
listen to radio shock jocks,
seldom read books,
and vote for stupid laws.
Their credo is the urban myth, with its siren song
of fatuous but plausible half-truth.
They believe themselves to be decent,
hard-working and honest (and often are)
it's what makes them so invincible.
But they're afraid of the dark,
and fearful of what they cannot understand.
And what they fear they learn to hate.
And what they hate they try to destroy.
They'd be a joke if not for the fact
that their collective voice usually
decides who runs the country.
They're impervious to reason or example;
try telling them they're wrong; that the way
they do things is not how civilisation works,
and they'll tell you to piss off; accuse you
of being a Chardonnay socialist, a bleeding heart,
or part of some intellectual elite
that wouldn't know its arse from its elbow.
These people are untouchable. They rule the world.

The White-faced Heron

Pale and sleek with eerie grace
he passes by in slender face.
And as he moves he seems to share
a depth of silence lingering there;
suggesting we are all involved
with this great labyrinth yet unsolved.
What unseen vision does he bring?
Whose pages do *his* stories sing?
And does he sense the higher sky
that cloaks my elevated eye?
In which context do we meet?
What confluence guides our passing feet?

He knows I watch him; I can see
the secret ways he watches me.

The Garden Studio at Varuna

(For Eleanor Dark)

Writing breaks the frozen sea within us,
Kafka told me long ago;
dragging this perilous moment
from the past
as scattered pages faintly breathe
upon her desk.
Giving up the hesitant, half-reluctant
light of drifting icebergs,
like some lost cause
in search of true believers.
On the wall her image gazes
calmly at the window,
but her husband's eyes are staring
straight at me,
with sceptical if not querulous intent.
Why are you here? he seems to ask.
To break the ice? I offer in reply.
Worrying my novel like a dog
at the unburied bone
before the frozen sea
returns again;
deeper than even Kafka
might have dreamt.

This poem was written in 1993 during a residential fellowship at Varuna, Eleanor Dark's old house in Katoomba, NSW, which is – thanks to the generosity of her son Mick – a writers' retreat.

Benediction

For Brian Cooper

We rest on sun-kissed stone a mountain high;
above Tilba Valley green and wide,
as a pair of eagles chase the sky,
like gods upon a rising tide.

We watch them fall through shining light,
wings outstretched and talons furled;
below us in their golden flight,
beyond the boundaries of our world.

They twist and fall and rise again,
a glorious swoop of rushing grace,
then dwindle on a distant plain,
inside the beauty of the place.

We retrace our steps down off the peak,
in single file with thoughts alone.
Knowing we will always seek
the memory of that sun-kissed stone.

The Mountain and the Eagle

In liquid light on wooded slopes,
Gulaga is weeping:
A Henry Moore sculpture
of a woman sleeping.
An eagle on the updraft
from Wallaga's sandy mouth,
mocks the law of gravity
with breezes from the south.
Waves curl towards the entrance
in question marks of foam;
the mountain and the eagle
are redefining home.
Flags of myth and moment,
and culture gathered wide,
shape a new republic's anxious hopes
from symbols of her pride.
But Gulaga's ancient valleys
whisper secrets of their own;
beyond the pale of history
and chilling to the bone.
The eagle falls with blurring speed;
dark blood rips the prey,
and dreaming in the sunlight,
bright shadows rim the bay.

The Need To Want

With apologies to Lewis Carroll

'Please tell me,' asked the Walrus,
as he ate another shrimp,
'what we had for breakfast,
and why it was so limp?'
'We had oysters,' said the Carpenter,
'and they were firm and fat,
you remarked as much your very self,
before you chased the cat.'
'Oh dear,' replied the Walrus,
eager to sound chaste,
'what's the point of oysters,
if you can't recall the taste?'
'Precisely,' said the Carpenter,
with a weary smile.
'To eat your share was wasteful –
to eat mine as well was vile.'
And then they rambled slowly home,
more in want than need,
reflecting on the way things are,
in a wonderland of greed.

A Rose By Any Other Name

Foot or finger, moon or stone,
rainbow, ribbon, spoon or bone.
Pour yourself a glass of wine
and listen to some Rubinstein.
All things exist without the name
that we invented with a game
inside the amber of its moat
to trap the words we learn by rote,
and make it difficult to see
the texture of reality.

The Final Straw

(For the Gatekeepers)

I've fallen out of love with poetry –
the trouble is, I'm not sure
who fell first: the singer or the song.

When young, I'd fallen in love with words;
seduced by the naivety of lilting reason –
before such humble joy was deconstructed
by linguistic Frisbees from a clever class.

Back then, I sought to engage poetry –
not by muffling the canon –
but trying to humanise imagination
with the healing balm of empathy –
A final straw I continue to clutch;
for reasons now barely remembered.

Moving On

The litmus poem,
at this late stage,
is dwindling
to an empty page.

Acknowledgements

As was the case with the 2001 edition of *Evening at Murunna Point*, I would like to acknowledge that this 2016 revised and expanded edition for the digital age makes use of previously published material. The lines I use as an epigraph come – with kind permission – from Cliff Hanna's book *Jock – A life story of John Shaw Neilson*, first published by UQP in 1999. My short story dedicated to the memory of Randolph Stow, 'The Frozen Sea', was first published in *The Canberra Times*, and I gratefully acknowledge the permission received from Stow's literary estate to use references and quotes from *To the Islands* and *A Counterfeit Silence*.

I choose to avoid digital social media, and have never been inclined (or, I suspect, able) to promote my own work in the manner required of writers today. And this – together with the fact that my writing, in topic as well as style, tends to lack an easily puffed commercial edge – has helped keep me in the literary shadows, despite having been published in the mainstream and winning several awards.

Living with the frustration and disappointment of being routinely overlooked and ignored has trapped me inside the tragic dilemma of a writer who needs to write, but doesn't want to in a system where context is likely to be seen as having greater relevance than text. And I would like to thank Brenda and Stephen Matthews for the intellectual honesty and creative empathy of their independent publishing journey, Ginninderra Press, which celebrated its twentieth year in 2016.

All my writing has had to achieve its expression through the malignant crucible of clinical depression and anxiety disorder, and while I am willing to concede the possibility that neither my writing nor my illness would exist as they do if separated from each other, their conjunction has taken a heavy toll, the effects of which have filtered through to my family and a few close friends. And for this unintended latter consequence, I extend an offer of sincere regret, along with gratitude for having stayed the course. Thank you.

www.ingramcontent.com/pod-product-compliance
Lightning Source LLC
Chambersburg PA
CBHW020334110726
47898CB00003B/867

* 9 7 8 1 7 6 0 4 1 2 9 2 0 *